YOUR SPIRITUAL GIFTS

YOUR
SPIRITUAL
GIFTS

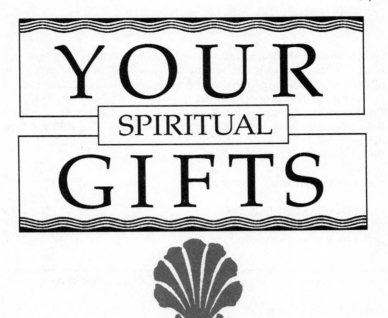

DONALD HOHENSEE
ALLEN ODELL

VICTOR BOOKS
A DIVISION OF SCRIPTURE PRESS PUBLICATIONS INC.
USA CANADA ENGLAND

Copyediting: Barbara Williams

Cover Design: Mardelle Ayres

Cover Illustration: Mardelle Ayres

Library of Congress Cataloging-in-Publication Data

Hohensee, Donald, 1939–
    Your spiritual gifts / by Donald Hohensee & Allen Odell.
        p.   cm.
    Includes bibliographical references.
    ISBN 0-89693-069-6
    1. Christian life — 1960- 2. Lay ministry. 3. Fruit of the Spirit.
    4. Self-actualization (Psychology) — Religious aspects — Christianity.
    I. Odell, Allen. II. Title.
    BV4501.2.H538 1992
    234'.13–dc20   92-9445
                                                                                       CIP

---

1   2   3   4   5   6   7   8   9   10   Printing/Year   96   95   94   93   92

DEDICATED TO

Norene L. Hohensee and
Eleanor L. Odell

ACKNOWLEDGMENTS

Many people made significant contributions to us, and we wish to recognize them.

This writing project began as a request by the Pacific Conference of the Evangelical Church for material compatible with its theological and biblical heritage. We thank Cliff Bergland and the Board of Evangelism for the confidence they invested in us.

Sally Brown and Kerrie Gross took our handwritten material and typed the early drafts. The original computer material went through several revisions, but we were able to work with the floppies they prepared. Thanks.

This material was taught to several hundred people in churches in the Northwest as well as in our classes at Western Evangelical Seminary. These people, too numerous to name, caused us to sharpen our thinking and refine our writing. We appreciate the correction that comes from the body of believers.

Student research scholars; Jim Taggart, Peter Lim, and Dannie Brown have read the material, checked our quotes, and assisted us in many ways. Dale Hauser helped with graphics and critiqued the material.

Our colleagues at WES have been of tremendous encouragement. William H. Vermillion pushed us to get this material published for wider circulation. Pat Rushford helped with her writing skills and encouragement.

We thank the Charles E. Fuller Institute of Evangelism and Church Growth, copyright holder of the "Wesley Spiritual Gifts Questionnaire," for the privilege to print it.

We thank Mark O. Sweeney, Vice President and Publisher of Victor Books, and his staff for their assistance.

Most of all, we thank God for the gifts and abilities He has given to us.

CONTENTS

LIST OF ILLUSTRATIONS

FOREWORD

One of Martin Luther's great gifts to the body of Christ was his rediscovery of the biblical concept of the priesthood of all believers. Previously the church had fallen into the false teaching that ordinary Christians did not have clear personal access to the Father without the aid of intermediaries called priests. Those of us who are heirs of the Reformation now take the priesthood of all believers virtually for granted, knowing that through Jesus Christ we do have individual access to God's throne.

However, Martin Luther did not carry the doctrine of the priesthood of all believers forward to include also the *ministry* of all believers. For that matter neither did John Calvin nor John Knox nor John Wesley. So far as ministry in the churches was concerned, our tradition has allowed a good bit of pre-Reformation clericalism to continue, although in a different form. Our classical theologians simply did not see that the Bible's teachings on spiritual gifts had a direct application as to how the ministry was to be done in the local congregation. Ministers for the most part continued to do the bulk of the ministry.

This changed drastically in the twentieth century. The first signs of change came with the advent of the Pentecostal movement around the turn of the century. However, strange as it may seem, even though Pentecostals began to stress certain spiritual gifts as available to all believers, the clericalism so typical of churches in general did not change that much. Pentecostal pastors, like Baptist and Methodist and Presbyterian pastors, continued doing most of the ministry of the churches and members were largely recipients of the ministry and spectators.

When I graduated from seminary in the mid 1950s, I had received virtually no teaching on spiritual gifts either in the curriculum or on the side. Today there is scarcely a seminary whose graduates are not aware of at least the basics about spiritual gifts and how they apply to the ministry of the laity.

My good friend, Donald Hohensee, is one who was among the first to sense this relatively new wind of the Holy Spirit blowing through our churches. He and his colleague, Allen Odell, have been teaching on spiritual gifts as the basis for the ministry of the laity for years. Now, for the first time, the crucial biblical insights which Don and Allen have discerned, their wealth of experience, and their wisdom and sensitivity in applying the teachings are made available to Christians everywhere in the excellent book you have in your hands.

It has been many years since we have been blessed with a new and exciting book about spiritual gifts. This one is particularly good because it is so practical. Not only is it designed to help you discover which gift or gifts God has given to you personally, but also, it does what other books fail to do and shows how your gifts and those of others can be used in the specific ministry areas of your local congregation.

This book will bless pastors. It will bless laypeople. And as it blesses both clergy and laity, it will bless churches as a whole. It is a wonderful resource which can be used individually, in study groups, in Sunday School classes, and in other areas of church life. As you discover your spiritual gift or gifts, you will be a better person and better able to serve God. And as many others in your church also discover their gifts, your church will be a brighter lighthouse in your community for the glory of God!

C. Peter Wagner
Fuller Theological Seminary
Pasadena, California

CHAPTER 1

Benefits of Knowing Your Gifts

T om walked down the aisle of the airplane in spiritual turmoil. When he entered the plane for the flight from Chicago to Los Angeles he had high expectations. The pastor of a large church had challenged him with his experience in soul-winning. "I always win my seatmate to faith in Christ," he said. Surely Tom could do the same.

At the check-in counter Tom surveyed the crowd. Who would sit next to him? He continued to wonder as he boarded the plane. When it seemed no one would, Tom felt a mixture of relief and disappointment. Then at the last minute a casually dressed businessman hurried down the aisle to take the empty seat. Tom's heart skipped a beat as he prayed, "Dear Lord, help me to be a good witness to this man." The plane door closed as the businessman was taking his seat. The stewardess stood holding her oxygen mask high in an effort to get their attention.

"Good afternoon," Tom said.

The businessman grunted in response.

"It's a beautiful day in the Windy City," Tom continued.

He gave a benign smile, pulled a large computer printout from his attaché case, buried himself in reading it, and made notes.

Well, maybe the man across the aisle would respond. Alas, he was already asleep. Tom's hopes rekindled when the stewardess woke him for his meal, but he didn't even finish his dinner before he was back to sleep.

Tom thought maybe he could talk to some of the men standing near the kitchen where drinks were being sold. As he approached, they all returned to their seats. *What is wrong with me?* Tom wondered. *Why can't I reach people like my pastor friend?*

Do you understand Tom's spiritual turmoil?

Maybe your experience differs. You know you are a Christian. You are faithful in attending your local church. You support the church with your tithes and offerings. You pray for the church. But you feel you should do more. God has blessed the pastoral staff with gifts and abilities. You may ask, "Are they the only ones God has gifted? I'm a layperson, does God have anything for me?"

Indeed he does.

This book is designed:

—to help you come to a biblical understanding of spiritual giftedness.

—to help you discover your spiritual gifts.

—to give you a brief historical perspective on gifts.

—to define the twenty-six gifts found in this study.

—to show how gifts can be employed in the local church.

When I started my study on spiritual gifts, I wanted to know how God had gifted me. I worked my way through a questionnaire designed for that purpose and was excited about what I found. I learned why I enjoyed teaching and administration; God had gifted me in those areas. I also learned why I was uncomfortable with music and exhortation; they were not part of my gift mix.

A spiritual gifts questionnaire to help you discover your gift mix follows this chapter. Remember it is an experience-based instrument. It is not an aptitude test but is designed to measure your degree of satisfaction in the things you do for the Lord.

If you are a young Christian with only a limited amount of experience, fill out the questionnaire based on your interests or what you think you'd like to do. Instead of reading, "In my life I have satisfactorily experienced. . . . " Read, "In my life I'd like to. . . ." This will give you an indication of your interests. You will then try out those areas in which you score high to see if that is indeed the way God has gifted you.

We will examine the Bible in chapter 2 to discover the gifts found in Scripture and the principles which affect the use of gifts. We attempt to lift these out as we examine the biblical passages.

A brief examination of the historical development of spiritual gifts in the church follows the biblical review. Within the church we found a broad range of theological perspectives. We have attempted to identify the larger segments and how they view spiritual gifts. Our perspective is Wesleyan, but we have identified other major views in regard to spiritual gifts.

As we conducted spiritual gifts seminars, we found confusion in several areas. How do spiritual gifts differ from the gift of the Holy Spirit? Is there a distinction between the fruit of the Spirit and His gifts? Do my natural talents become spiritual gifts after I'm converted? Are there some expectations of me just because I'm a Christian which are no indication of spiritual giftedness? How many gifts do I receive? We attempt to answer these questions in chapter 4.

Chapters 5, 6, and 7 discuss the twenty-six gifts we identified in Scripture. We have divided the gifts into three categories: Enabling Gifts, Serving Gifts, and Sign Gifts.

In chapter 8 we suggest things you can do to assist in the discovery of your spiritual gifts. Do these things in light of your findings based on the questionnaire you completed earlier. The discovery and use of spiritual gifts are part of Christian growth and maturity.

We believe that gifts are given to serve the body of Christ rather than for mere personal satisfaction. Gifts are recognized by that group and there they are used. We believe that the local church is the best expression of the body. In chapter 9 we show that gifts and their use will reflect the philosophy of ministry of the local church.

Spiritual gifts were never designed for you to tell the church what it should do. Rather, the local church determines the ministries which are needed. They call individuals to be involved in those ministries. The local church then gives those people authority to minister.

Chapter 11 discusses how the local church can organize or structure itself for ministry based on spiritual gifts.

The final chapter is a call to commitment. As we examine Moses' life, we see that God had no problem with Moses' inadequacies. Rather, God reacted in anger over Moses' unwillingness to serve. God is waiting and wanting our commitment.

This book began as a request from a group of pastors for material they could use in their churches. We first designed it to be a series of lessons which could be taught in a Sunday School class or other classtime. As we conducted seminars, we discovered that not everyone could be in a class and so revised this material for the individual to use. We believe the present material can be used either way.

Don Hohensee is primarily responsible for the first eight chapters, Allen Odell for the last four. In preparing this material we frequently went to a restaurant for a cup of coffee and for the opportunity to interact with each other. Traveling to seminars gave us other times to expound our ideas and discuss the implications of the things we were learning. It also gave us an opportunity to reflect on the responses of the people in the seminars. In many ways both of us are involved throughout the book.

Allen Odell pastored for fifteen years and has served as a Conference Director of Christian Education for seven years. Don Hohensee was a missionary in Burundi, East Africa for fifteen years. Both of us have been professors at Western Evangelical Seminary since 1980.

 DISCUSSION

1. Make a list of three questions you want answered about spiritual gifts as you read this book.
2. List three goals you would like to reach as a result of reading this book.
3. As you read this book keep your local church in mind.

 APPLICATION

Find a friend to read this book with you. Then you will have someone to discuss your insights with as you work through the discussion questions.

QUESTIONNAIRE
Wesley Spiritual Gifts

The Wesley Spiritual Gifts Questionnaire gives you a handle on what your spiritual gift(s) might be. It is adapted from earlier spiritual gifts evaluations, copyrighted 1978, 1981, 1982, by the Fuller Evangelistic Association, P.O. Box 91990, Pasadena, CA 91109-1990. The questionnaire was originally designed by Richard F. Houts (*Eternity*, May 1976, pp. 18–21). It was later revised by Dr. C. Peter Wagner and became known as the "Wagner Modified Houts Questionnaire." A further revision, known as the "Trenton Spiritual Gifts Analysis," was developed and used at St. Paul Lutheran Church in Trenton, Michigan. The "Wesley Spiritual Gifts Questionnaire" was adapted by Donald Hohensee of Western Evangelical Seminary, Portland, Oregon for use in churches of the Wesleyan-Arminian persuasion.

To reorder this item, ask for C110. Charles E. Fuller Institute of Evangelism and Church Growth, P.O. Box 91990, Pasadena, CA 91109-1990, (818) 449-0425. Outside California call 1 (800) CFULLER. This is copyrighted material and cannot be reproduced in any form.

As you begin the process of discovering your spiritual gift(s), keep in mind that the results will show how you are equipped to serve the Lord, helping to build up the church, the body of Christ, to a position of strength and maturity, to the point of being filled fully with Christ.

Instructions
1. Go through the list of 120 statements on the Wesley Spiritual Gifts Questionnaire. For each one, say to yourself: "In my life I have satisfactorily experienced. . . ." and

then check the appropriate box: "Much," "Some," "Little," or "None."

2. When you are finished, follow the instructions for scoring the questionnaire given on page 31.

3. Next, looking at the "Total" column of the Wesley Spiritual Gifts Chart on page 32, enter *below* in the "Dominant" section the three gifts on which you received the highest scores. Then enter in the "Subordinate" section the next three highest scoring gifts. This will give you a *tentative* evaluation of where your gifts may lie.

Dominant: 1. _____

                2. _____

                3. _____

Subordinate: 1. _____

                2. _____

                3. _____

This inventory is based on your past experiences. If you are over thirty or have been a Christian ten years or more (and beyond your teen years), then you should only deal with what you have already experienced.

If you are under thirty or have been a Christian less than ten years, you may want to do this exam based on your interests. Be fair in evaluating your interests—do you really feel that way or do you just think you should? If you base your answer on interests, you will need to go out and test the results. Remember, the true test of a spiritual gift is your effectiveness and subjective feelings as you use it as well as confirmation from other believers.

As you read each statement say to yourself: "In my life I have satisfactorily experienced. . . . "

Benefits of Knowing Your Gifts

"In my life I have satisfactorily experienced . . . "

	MUCH (3)	SOME (2)	LITTLE (1)	NONE (0)
1 Proclaiming the truth of God in an inspired and enthusiastic manner.	3			
2 Having responsibility for the growth of a group of Christians.	3			
3 Adapting well in a different culture in order to evangelize.	3			
4 Leading other people to a decision for salvation through faith in Christ.	3			
5 Speaking words of encouragement to those who are troubled, discouraged, or not sure of themselves.	3			
6 Finding pleasure in the drawing and/or designing of various objects.			1	
7 Applying truth effectively in my life.	3			
8 Being able to help other people learn biblical facts and details which aid in the building up of their lives.	3			
9 Seeing the difference between truth and error.	3			
10 Having the ability to discover new truths for myself.	3			
11 Knowing that the repair and maintenance of things in my environment comes easily to me.			1	

	MUCH	SOME	LITTLE	NONE
"In my life I have satisfactorily experienced . . . "	(3)	(2)	(1)	(0)
12 Managing money well in order to give liberally to the work of the Lord.		2		
13 Assisting key leaders to relieve them for their essential jobs.	3			
14 Providing food and/or lodging graciously and willingly to people who are in need.		2		
15 Joyfully singing praises to God either alone or with other people.	3			
16 Praying for other people and often losing track of the time.	3			
17 Persuading other people to accomplish present goals and objectives.	3			
18 Working joyfully with and helping those people who are ignored by the majority of others around them.	3			
19 Believing God will keep His promises in spite of circumstances.	3			
20 Being able to discern when to delegate important responsibility, and to whom.	3			
21 Being able to effectively play a musical instrument.				0

Benefits of Knowing Your Gifts

	MUCH (3)	SOME (2)	LITTLE (1)	NONE (0)
"In my life I have satisfactorily experienced . . ."				
22 Enjoying the fact that I am called on to do special jobs.	3			
23 Being able to glorify God by miraculously changing circumstances through the name of the Lord.	3			
24 Being able, in the name of the Lord, to bring help to physical afflictions.	3			
25 Preaching the Word of God in a manner that brings conviction to the hearers.	3			
26 Sacrificially giving myself for infant or straying Christians.	3			
27 Learning another language well to help start a church.				0
28 Sharing joyfully with other people how Jesus has brought me to Himself.	3			
29 Being an instrument for dislodging the careless and redirecting the wayward to face spiritual realities.	3			
30 Finding joy in painting pictures or in making handcrafted objects.				0
31 Being able to intuitively reach good solutions to complicated problems.	3			

"In my life I have satisfactorily experienced . . . "

	MUCH (3)	SOME (2)	LITTLE (1)	NONE (0)
32 Enjoying the times I share my biblical knowledge and the knowledge of others with children and/or adults.	3			
33 Judging well between the evil and the good.	3			
34 Knowing that the insights I possess and share with other people will bring change in attitude and conviction to my fellow Christians.	3			
35 Working with various manual projects and enjoying it.			1	
36 Giving my money and/or things liberally to the work of the Lord.	3			
37 Helping in small ways that oftentimes seem to be behind the scenes.	3			
38 Enjoying having guests in my home.			1	
39 Leading others in singing songs of praise to God or for pure enjoyment.	3			
40 Finding myself praying when I could be doing other things.	3			
41 Leading Christian followers in a clear direction.	3			

"In my life I have satisfactorily experienced . . ."	MUCH (3)	SOME (2)	LITTLE (1)	NONE (0)
42 Talking cheerfully with the elderly, the shut-in person, or those in jails or prisons.		2		
43 Having a conviction of the reality of an active God in the daily affairs of my local church.	3			
44 Being able to organize ideas, people, things, and time for more effective ministry.	3			
45 Being involved in a church, school, or local musical instrumental presentation.		2		0
46 Enjoying routine work at church that would seemingly bore other people.	3			
47 Being empowered by the Spirit to expel demons in the name of the Lord.	3			
48 Being able to bring healing to the emotionally sick.	3			
49 Communicating great truths of God in a gripping, compelling, clear fashion, clearly spoken from the Lord.	3			
50 Knowing and being well known to the same group of people over an extended period of time, and sharing with them in successes and failures.	3			

"In my life I have satisfactorily experienced . . ."	MUCH (3)	SOME (2)	LITTLE (1)	NONE (0)
51 Being able to begin new churches with a different language and culture.				0
52 Enjoying meeting other people and sharing with them the joy and peace which Jesus and His love have given me.	3			
53 Verbally challenging the spiritually apathetic.	3			
54 Finding joy in having a beautiful lawn, flowers, and shrubs which are properly placed and cared for.				0
55 Choosing from alternatives an option which usually works.	3			
56 Making difficult biblical truths understandable to others.	3			
57 Having insights into the motives of people and being able to see beneath the surface.	3			
58 Acquiring and mastering new facts and principles which can be applied to given situations to aid others in their growth and stability.	3			
59 Enjoying the work necessary for gardening, landscaping, and other projects.				0

	MUCH	SOME	LITTLE	NONE
"In my life I have satisfactorily experienced . . ."	(3)	(2)	(1)	(0)
60 Cheerfully giving so that God's work can be extended and helped.	3			
61 Typing, filing, or recording figures or minutes necessary in the work of the Lord.			1	
62 Having guests and/or visitors in my presence and making them feel welcome and a part of things.	3			
63 Singing familiar Gospel songs with groups of fellow Christians or as solos.			1	
64 Taking prayer requests very seriously and praying until the answer comes.	3			
65 Having others follow me and the example I set because I have knowledge which contributes to the building of my church.	3			
66 Visiting in hospitals and/or retirement homes and knowing that my presence has helped in comforting and cheering those people with whom I have come in contact.	3			
67 Trusting in the presence and power of God for the impossible.	3			

	MUCH	SOME	LITTLE	NONE
"In my life I have satisfactorily experienced . . . "	(3)	(2)	(1)	(0)
68 Planning and administering programs which benefit my fellow Christians.	3			
69 Using my instrumental music talents for the appreciation of my friends and to the glory of God.				0
70 Feeling satisfaction in doing menial tasks for the glory of God.		2		
71 Seeing God intervene and doing the impossible in my life.	3			
72 Being used by God to treat successfully those who are spiritually sick.	3			
73 Preaching effectively so as to help people reach a verdict and respond to God.	3			
74 Feeding followers by guiding them to selected portions of the Bible.	3			
75 Being able to relate well to Christians of a different race, language, or culture.		2		
76 Seeking out unbelievers in a continual manner in order to win them for Jesus.	3	2		
77 Being able to effectively counsel those people who are perplexed or confused, guilty or addicted.	3			

26

"In my life I have satisfactorily experienced . . ."	MUCH (3)	SOME (2)	LITTLE (1)	NONE (0)
78 Enjoying the times that I am able to create beautiful items especially when they benefit others.			1	
79 Having my nominations of certain people for church positions prove to be good selections.		2		
80 Training Christians to be obedient disciples of Christ.	3			
81 Being able to identify ideas, plans, or activities that are not true to the Bible.	3			
82 Reading and studying a great deal in order to build myself up in the understanding of biblical truths.	3			
83 Finding out that my skills in building or repairing objects benefit others.				0
84 Feeling deeply moved when confronted with urgent financial needs in the work of God's kingdom.		2		
85 Being happy when others get credit for what I do.		2		
86 Opening my home to visiting preachers and/or missionaries and sharing with them what I have.				0

"In my life I have satisfactorily experienced . . . "

	MUCH (3)	SOME (2)	LITTLE (1)	NONE (0)
87 Finding much joy and pleasure in the seemingly simple routine of singing hymns and other Gospel selections.	3			
88 Feeling when I am asked to pray for others that my prayers will have tangible results. *FAITH*	3			
89 Being able to lead small or large groups of people in decision-making processes.	3			
90 Helping other people without expecting them to do anything in return.	3			
91 Being confident that God will bring victory into difficult situations even when others are discouraged.	3			
92 Being able to set goals and objectives and then to make plans to reach or accomplish them.	3			
93 Finding that my ability to perform instrumental music has helped others grow as Christians.				0
94 Being ready to take orders rather than give them.	3			
95 Being an instrument of God's supernatural change in lives or events.	3			

"In my life I have satisfactorily experienced . . . "	MUCH (3)	SOME (2)	LITTLE (1)	NONE (0)
96 Praying for others that healing might happen.	3			
97 Bringing messages that cut to the heart.	3			
98 Bringing back into the fold of God those who have wandered away.	3			
99 Having the ability to learn foreign languages.				0
100 Continually going where unbelievers are in order to win them.	3	2		
101 Comforting a Christian in his/her affliction or suffering.	3			
102 Receiving much joy from working with my hands at various arts and crafts.			1	
103 Having an unusual sense of the presence of God and personal confidence when important decisions needed to be made.	3			
104 Sharing my knowledge of the love of Christ with children and/or adults in an effective and meaningful manner.	3			
105 Seeing through a phony before his/her phoniness is clearly evident.	3			

"In my life I have satisfactorily experienced . . ."	MUCH (3)	SOME (2)	LITTLE (1)	NONE (0)
106 Distinguishing important biblical truths that benefit myself and others as members of the body of Christ.	3			
107 Enjoying maintenance and repair work around the church facilities.				0
108 Being ready to forego certain privileges in order to give money to God's work.		2		
109 Finding joy in being an aide to someone who can use my help and concern.	3			
110 Inviting visitors and guests (strangers) home to dinner after Sunday morning worship.				0
111 Singing as one of my favorite spiritual exercises.	3			
112 Praying as one of my favorite spiritual exercises.	3			
113 Being able to motivate other people to become involved in the building up of the church.	3			
114 Comforting a fellow Christian during sickness or times of problems and/or anxiety.	3			
115 Trusting in the reliability of God when all else looks dim.	3			

	MUCH	SOME	LITTLE	NONE
"In my life I have satisfactorily experienced . . . "	(3)	(2)	(1)	(0)
116 Knowing where to place Christians so they can exercise their spiritual gifts.	3			
117 Playing a musical instrument as a helpful spiritual exercise for myself.				0
118 Enjoying it when others express a need for my help.	3			
119 Having God work through my life and often doing impossible things.	3			
120 Seeing God heal someone in direct answer to my prayers.	3			

WESLEY SPIRITUAL GIFTS CHART

Instructions

In the grid on the following page, enter the numerical value of each of your responses next to the number of the corresponding statements on the preceding pages.

Much = 3   Some = 2   Little = 1   None = 0

Now add up the five numbers that you have recorded in each row, placing the sum in the "Total" column.

Determine your gift-mix by circling the three gifts on which you received the highest scores. These are in all probability your dominant gifts. Place a check by the next three highest; these are your subordinate gifts. With this in mind, begin to test out these gifts by attempting to use them systematically.

Your Spiritual Gifts

10/93

ROWS	VALUE OF ANSWERS					TOTAL		GIFT
Row A	1	25	49	73	97	15	✓	Prophecy
Row B	2	26	50	74	98	15	✓	Pastor
Row C	3 3	27 0	51 0	75 2	99 0	5		Missionary
Row D	4	28	52	76	100	13		Evangelism
Row E	5	29	53	77	101	15	✓	Exhortation
Row F	6 1	30 0	54 0	78 1	102 1	3		Craftsmanship/ Artistic
Row G	7 3	31 3	55 3	79 2	103 3	14		Wisdom
Row H	8	32	56	80	104	15	✓	Teaching
Row I	9	33	57	81	105	15	✓	Discernment of Spirits
Row J	10	34	58	82	106	15	✓	Knowledge
Row K	11 1	35 1	59 0	83 0	107 0	2		Craftsmanship/ Manual
Row L	12 2	36 3	60 3	84 2	108 2	12		Giving
Row M	13 2	37 3	61 1	85 2	109 3	12		Helps
Row N	14 2	38 1	62 3	86 0	110 0	6		Hospitality
Row O	15 3	39 3	63 1	87 3	111 3	13		Music/ Vocal
Row P	16	40	64	88	112	15	✓	Prayer
Row Q	17	41	65	89	113	15	✓	Leadership
Row R	18	42 2	66	90	114	14		Mercy
Row S	19	43	67	91	115	15	✓	Faith
Row T	20	44	68	92	116	15	✓	Administration
Row U	21 0	45 0	69 0	93 0	117 0	0		Music/ Instrumental
Row V	22 3	46 2	70 2	94 3	118 3	14		Service
Row W	23 3	47 3	71 3	95 3	119 3	15	✓	Miracles
Row X	24 3	48 3	72 3	96 3	120 3	15	✓	Healing

REVIEW OF GIFT DEFINITIONS
AND SCRIPTURE REFERENCES

The following pages contain suggested definitions of the spiritual gifts. While not meant to be dogmatic or final, these definitions and supporting Scriptures do correspond to characteristics of the gifts as expressed in the **Wesley Spiritual Gifts Questionnaire.**

A. *Prophecy.* The gift of prophecy is the special ability that God gives to certain members of the body of Christ to proclaim the Word of God with divine unction which brings conviction to the hearers so they recognize that it is truly the Word of God and that they must do something about it.	Acts 2:37-40 Acts 7:54 Acts 17:32-34 Acts 26:24-29 1 Thes. 1:5 1 Cor. 14:1, 3
B. *Pastor.* The gift of pastor is the special ability that God gives to certain members of the body of Christ to assume a long-term personal responsibility for the spiritual welfare of a group of believers.	1 Tim. 3:1-7 John 10:1-18 1 Peter 5:1-3 Eph. 4:11-14
C. *Missionary.* The gift of missionary is the special ability that God gives to certain members of the body of Christ to minister whatever other spiritual gifts they have in a second culture.	1 Cor. 9:19-23 Acts 8:4 Acts 13:2-3 Acts 22:21 Rom. 10:15
D. *Evangelism.* The gift of evangelism is the special ability that God gives to certain members of the body of Christ to share the Gospel with unbelievers	Eph. 4:11-14 2 Tim. 4:5 Acts 8:5-6, 26-40 Acts 14:21

in such a way that men and women become Jesus' disciples and responsible members of the body of Christ.

Acts 21:8

E. *Exhortation.* The gift of exhortation is the special ability that God gives to certain members of the body of Christ to minister words of comfort, consolation, encouragement, and counsel to other members of the body in such a way that they feel helped and healed.

Rom. 12:8
1 Tim. 4:13
Heb. 10:25
Acts 14:22

F. *Craftsmanship/Artistic.* The gift of craftsmanship is the special ability to use your hands, thoughts, and mind to further the kingdom of God through artistic, creative means. People with this gift may also serve as leaders for others in forming their abilities in this area. The gift may also be used in the areas of maintenance, care, and upkeep for the benefit and beautification of God's kingdom here on earth.

2 Chron. 34:9-13
Ex. 30:22-25
Ex. 31:3-11
Acts 16:14
Acts 18:3

G. *Wisdom.* The gift of wisdom is the special ability that God gives to certain members of the body of Christ to know the mind of the Holy Spirit in such a way as to receive insight into how given knowledge may best be applied to specific needs arising in the body of Christ.

1 Cor. 2:1-13
1 Cor. 12:8
Acts 6:3, 10
James 1:5-6
2 Peter 3:15

H. *Teaching.* The gift of teaching is the special ability that God gives to certain

1 Cor. 12:28
Eph. 4:11-14

| members of the body of Christ to communicate information relevant to the health and ministry of the body and its members in such a way that others will learn. | Rom. 12:7
Acts 18:24-28
Acts 20:20-21 |

I. *Discernment of Spirits.* The gift of discerning of spirits is the special ability that God gives to certain members of the body of Christ to know with assurance whether certain behavior purported to be of God is in reality divine, human, or satanic.

1 Cor. 12:10
Acts 5:1-11
Acts 16:16-18
1 John 4:1-6
Matt. 16:21-23

J. *Knowledge.* The gift of knowledge is the special ability that God gives to certain members of the body of Christ to discover, accumulate, analyze, and clarify information which is pertinent to the growth and well-being of the body.

1 Cor. 2:14
1 Cor. 12:8
Acts 5:1-11
Col. 2:2-3
2 Cor. 11:6

K. *Craftsmanship/Manual.* See F.

L. *Giving.* The gift of giving is the special ability that God gives to certain members of the body of Christ to contribute their material resources to the work of the Lord with liberality and cheerfulness.

Rom. 12:8
2 Cor. 8:1-7
2 Cor. 9:2-8
Mark 12:41-44

M. *Helps.* The gift of helps is the special ability that God gives to certain members of the body of Christ to invest the talents they have in the life and ministry of other members of the

1 Cor. 12:28
Rom. 16:1-2
Acts 9:36
Luke 8:2-3
Mark 15:40-41

body, thus enabling those others to increase the effectiveness of their own
spiritual gifts.

N. *Hospitality.* The gift of hospitality is
the special ability that God gives to
certain members of the body of Christ
to provide an open house and a warm
welcome to those in need of food and
lodging.

1 Peter 4:9
Rom. 12:9-13
Rom. 16:23
Acts 16:14-15
Heb. 13:1-2

O. *Music/Vocal.* The gift of music is the
special ability to use one's voice in the
singing of praises and joy to the Lord
for the benefit of others, or to play a
musical instrument to the praise of the
Lord and for the benefit of others.

1 Chron. 16:41-42
2 Chron. 5:12-13
2 Chron. 34:12
1 Sam. 16:16
Deut. 31:22
Ps. 150

P. *Prayer/Intercession.* The gift of
prayer/intercession is the special ability that God gives to certain members
of the body of Christ to pray for extended periods of time on a regular
basis and see frequent and specific answers to their prayers, to a degree
much greater than that which is expected of the average Christian.

James 5:14-16
1 Tim. 2:1-2
Col. 1:9-12
Col. 4:12-13
Acts 12:12
Luke 22:41-44

Q. *Leadership.* The gift of leadership is
the special ability that God gives to
certain members of the body of Christ
to set goals in accordance with God's
purpose for the future and to communicate those goals to others in such a
way that they voluntarily and harmo-

1 Tim. 5:17
Acts 7:10
Acts 15:7-11
Rom. 12:8
Heb. 13:17
Luke 9:51

niously work together to accomplish
those goals for the glory of God.

R. *Mercy.* The gift of mercy is the special ability that God gives to certain members of the body of Christ to feel genuine empathy and compassion for individuals (both Christian and non-Christian) who suffer distressing physical, mental, or emotional problems, and to translate that compassion into cheerfully done deeds which reflect Christ's love and alleviate the suffering.	Rom. 12:8 Mark 9:41 Acts 16:33-34 Luke 10:33-35 Matt. 20:29-34 Matt. 25:34-40 Acts 11:28-30
S. *Faith.* The gift of faith is the special ability that God gives to certain members of the body of Christ to discern with extraordinary confidence the will and purposes of God for His work.	1 Cor. 12:9 Acts 11:22-24 Acts 27:21-25 Heb. 11 Rom. 4:18-21
T. *Administration.* The gift of administration is the special ability that God gives to certain members of the body of Christ to understand clearly the immediate and long-range goals of a particular unit of the body of Christ and to devise and execute plans for the accomplishment of those goals.	1 Cor. 12:28 Acts 6:1-7 Acts 27:11 Luke 14:28-30
U. *Music/Instrumental.* See O.	
V. *Service.* The gift of service is the special ability that God gives to certain members of the body of Christ to identify the unmet needs involved in a	2 Tim. 1:16-18 Rom. 12:7 Acts 6:1-7 Titus 3:14

task related to God's work, and to make use of available resources to meet those needs and help accomplish the desired results.	Gal. 6:2, 10
W. *Miracles.* The gift of miracles is the special ability that God gives to certain members of the body of Christ to serve as human intermediaries through whom it pleases God to perform powerful acts that are perceived by observers to have altered the ordinary course of nature.	1 Cor. 12:10, 28 Acts 9:36-42 Acts 19:11-20 Acts 20:7-12 Rom. 15:18-19 2 Cor. 12:12
X. *Healing.* The gift of healing is the special ability that God gives to certain members of the body of Christ to serve as human intermediaries through whom it pleases God to cure illness and restore health.	1 Cor. 12:9, 28 Acts 3:1-10 Acts 5:12-16 Acts 9:32-35 Acts 28:7-10

There are some other gifts mentioned or implied in Scripture which have not been included as part of the *Wesley Spiritual Gifts Questionnaire.* Definitions for those gifts are listed below.

AA. *Apostle.* The gift of apostle is the special ability that God gives to certain members of the body of Christ to assume and exercise general leadership over a number of churches with an extraordinary authority in spiritual matters which is spontaneously recognized and appreciated by those churches.	1 Cor. 12:28 2 Cor. 12:12 Eph. 4:11-14 Eph. 3:1-9 Acts 15:1-2 Gal. 2:7-10

BB. *Languages/Tongues.* The gift of languages is the special ability that God gives to certain members of the body of Christ to speak a divinely anointed message in a language they have never learned.

Acts 2:1-13
Acts 10:44-46
Acts 19:1-7
Mark 16:17

CC. *Interpretation.* The gift of interpretation is the special ability that God gives to certain members of the body of Christ to make known to listeners what another had said in a language different from the hearers. The interpreter may not have studied the language being interpreted.

1 Cor. 12:10, 30
1 Cor. 14:26-28

The following two gifts are not found in a gift list in the New Testament but have scriptural support.

DD. *Celibacy.* The gift of celibacy is the special ability that God gives to certain members of the body of Christ to remain single and enjoy it for the sake of Christ and not suffer undue sexual temptations.

1 Cor. 7:7-8
Matt. 19:10-12

EE. *Martyrdom.* The gift of martyrdom is the special ability that God gives to certain members of the body of Christ to undergo suffering for the faith even to the point of death, while consistently displaying a joyous and victorious attitude which brings glory to God.

1 Cor. 13:3
Acts 5:27-41
Acts 7:54-60
Acts 12:1-5
2 Cor. 11:21-30
2 Cor. 12:9-10

CHAPTER 2

A Good Foundation

Grace

BIBLICAL UNDERSTANDING OF GIFTS

Evangelical Christians want to examine the Word of God for its perspective on everything that affects us. We want to be anchored to the Word so we don't get off into false or misleading teaching. There are three main passages that deal with spiritual gifts — Romans 12:3-8; 1 Corinthians 12:1-11, 28; and Ephesians 4:11-16. We will examine each of these passages to find the gifts listed and to learn the principles Scripture lays out in regard to gifts. We will define each gift in later sections.

Paul refers to gifts in Greek as *charismata* (plural form of gifts; *charisma* is the singular). The root on which this word is built is *charis* — grace.

This helps in our understanding. All these gifts are graciously given by God. He is the source of the gifts; they are to be used for His service. They are gifts given by the grace of God.

41

ROMANS 12:3-8

Paul presents several principles that need to be kept in mind. First, a right understanding of one's gift will cause the person to have a balanced estimation of his/her place within the body (v. 3). The person will not have an exaggerated idea of his or her self-worth, nor a groveling feeling of his or her value. The person will be able to think correctly and have a sane self-estimation. There is no basis for pride; the gift is given by God. Nor is there a basis for false humility; God has gifted the individual.

A second principle Paul establishes is that in Christ all belong to one body (vv. 4-5). His comparison is to a human body with its many members. These members have different functions, but they work in harmony so the body can function as a unit. Likewise in Christ, we need each other because there is only one body. Some members cannot get along without the others. Each member belongs to the other members. We are all joined together in the body of Christ. While this principle has universal application and truth, it is most easily seen at the local level, the individual congregation. At this level we need each other; we need the entire family of God.

The third principle taught (v. 6) is that these gifts are given to us by grace. God in His great wisdom knows what is needed and so gives His gifts to His servants.

Paul lists several gifts (vv. 6-8): Prophecy, service, teaching, encouraging (exhortation), giving, leadership, and mercy. Whatever gift an individual receives, he/she should use that gift to the best of his/her ability.

1 CORINTHIANS 12:1-11, 28

The second section in which Paul discusses gifts is 1 Corinthians 12:1-11, 28. Actually chapters 12–14 of

1 Corinthians are a discussion on gifts. In this long section Paul gives several other principles in regard to the use of gifts.

Paul wanted the Corinthians to be informed correctly about spiritual matters (12:1). There is no merit for ignorance in the things of the Spirit. A second truth he establishes (vv. 4-6) is that while there are different kinds of gifts, different kinds of service, and different kinds of workings, there is only one God who is in charge of all of these variations. It is the one Holy Spirit who gives these for the common good of the body (vv. 7, 11). He gives these to each individual as He determines is best. In that sense God chooses what He knows to be best for each individual and what is needful for the body of Christ.

He then gives his first list in chapter 12: wisdom, knowledge, faith, healing, miracles, prophecy, discernment, languages, and interpretation.

All Parts Are Needed
Paul followed this with a long discussion (12:12-26) on the fact that each part of the body is needed. All belong to the body whether Jew or Gentile; all have received the same Holy Spirit. There is no part of the body that is unnecessary. Just because one part receives greater honor does not mean it is more important. Nor because another part has a lower place, in human estimation, that it is of lesser value. God has put the body together the way He felt was best. He created the body to have many members because He knew that would be the best arrangement. There is to be no division in the body. In the human body if one part hurts, the whole body hurts; if one part is honored, the whole body is honored. So it is to be in Christ. All members are needed, all gifts are necessary. While some people may have several gifts, no one has all the gifts, so we need each other.

Paul gives his second list in 1 Corinthians 12. They are apostles, prophets, teachers, miracle workers, healing, service, administration, languages, and interpretation. His use of questions in verses 29-30 suggests that no one has all the gifts.

Love Is above All the Gifts

In his great chapter on love (1 Cor. 13), Paul showed that gifts without love have no lasting value. If these gifts are exercised but there is no love present, they are worthless. If gifts cause division, they are out of divine order. Gifts will go out of existence, but fruit will remain — the fruit of love, joy, and peace. Love is to be the dominant attitude.

Paul continued his discussion of gifts in chapter 14. All are to follow the way of love and should desire spiritual things, especially that they might prophesy. In Paul's estimation the one who is prophesying is greater than the one speaking in a language unless he interprets. He then compared speaking in a language and prophesying. Languages have meaning to the speakers of those languages, but if I don't know the language, I'm a foreigner to that person and he to me. So Paul said, excel in gifts that build up the church.

Languages Are for Unbelievers

He continued his discussion by stating that languages are for unbelievers. In 1 Corinthians 14:21 he quoted from two Old Testament passages, Isaiah 28:11-12 and Deuteronomy 28:49. The context shows that God had already spoken to these peoples in languages they understood, but they refused to hearken. Because these people refused to obey God's repeated instructions to them in their mother tongue, He sent foreign armies to subjugate them. They would then know that what God had spoken to them through His prophets was indeed the truth. They would become believers when strangers subjugated them and commanded them in languages they did not know. Paul went on to show that prophecy is for believers and it will bring conviction to the unconverted (1 Cor. 14:24-25).

Worship is to be done in an orderly manner. Only two or three are to prophesy or speak in a language in a service. Interpretation must be present if languages are used. God does not create disorder and chaos in a service, rather He creates order and peace. All things are to be done in an orderly manner. Gifts need to be used in such a way that the church is strengthened and not divided.

EPHESIANS 4:11-16

The last main section on gifts is in Ephesians 4:11-16. Paul again discussed unity in the body of Christ. He showed (in v. 7) that each received grace according to Christ's discretion. He listed some of the gifted people God gave to the church. These include: apostles, prophets, evangelists, pastors, and teachers.

The purpose for these gifted persons is the edification of the church. They are to prepare God's people for service. They are to build up the body of Christ. They are to become mature believers filled with the fullness of Christ. They are no longer to be immature believers who are easily deceived. Rather they are to grow up in Christ. The body grows by being held together with all of the supporting muscles. It grows as each does its part.

OTHER GIFTS

We have looked at the three key passages with their teaching on gifts. Frequently the question arises, "Are these all the gifts?" It is our judgment that Paul has not intended for these lists to be exhaustive. Paul in 1 Corinthians 7:7 speaks of having the gift of celibacy which obviously not everyone else received.

We believe God worked through the Holy Spirit similarly in both Testaments. We can point to some gifted people in the Old Testament. God gifted Bezalel and Oholiab with craftsmanship so they could make all the things needful for the construction of the tabernacle (Ex. 31:1-11). At a later time there were others who were so gifted in the repair of the temple (2 Chron. 34:9-13).

God also gave gifted musicians who led the people in singing (Deut. 31:22; 1 Chron. 16:41-42). Others were gifted in the playing of musical instruments (16:42; 2 Chron. 5:12-13; Ps. 150).

C. Peter Wagner has a good argument for the gift of missionary in *Your Spiritual Gifts Can Help Your Church Grow*. These are those gifted people who can more easily minister cross-culturally than others do. More will be written on this in a later section.

Paul as a missionary used the gift of exorcism. One such occasion is recorded in Acts 16:16-18. Peter speaks of offering hospitality without complaining (1 Peter 4:9-10). This gift is to be used to serve others. He who does so shows God's grace in its variety of forms.

We have no desire to open up this discussion on spiritual gifts so that every ability known to mankind could be considered a spiritual gift; we do feel there is sufficient support in Scripture for the ones we have noted to add them to our presentation.

A comparison of the gifts, as found in the key "gift" passages and the other additions, is found on page 47.

The only gift that made all four of the main gift lists is prophecy. This is consistent with Paul's exhortation to the Corinthians that they should seek to prophesy. He obviously felt this was very important. Teaching made three of the lists. Service, healing, miracles, languages, interpre-

A Chart of Gifts in Scripture

Rom. 12:6-8	1 Cor. 12:1-11	1 Cor. 12:28-30	Eph. 4:11-16	Other Gifts
Prophecy	Prophecy	Prophecy	Prophecy	
Service		Service		
Teaching		Teaching	Teaching	
Encouragement				
Giving				
Leadership				
Mercy				
	Wisdom			
	Knowledge			
	Faith			
	Healing	Healing		
	Miracles	Miracles		
	Discernment			
	Languages	Languages		
	Interpretation	Interpretation		
		Apostleship	Apostleship	
		Administration		
			Evangelism	
			Pastors	
				Hospitality— 1 Peter 4:9-10
				Celibacy— 1 Cor. 7:7
				Craftsmanship— Ex. 31:1-11
				Music— 1 Chron. 16:41-42
				Missionary
				Exorcism— Acts 16:16-18
				Prayer— Col. 4:12-13

tation, and apostleship were mentioned twice. The principle we can draw from this is that the church needs a lot of people with the gifts of prophecy and teaching. But all the gifts have their place and are needful to the body.

The usage of the present tense suggests to us that these gifts are to be in operation today. God gave these gifts and gifted individuals to the church in the Apostolic Age, but He continues to give these gifts to other people today so the body of Christ can function as it ought.

We trust that this study on gifts will prove to be an exciting study for you personally as well as for the church if this material is used in a teaching situation. We trust that it shall be a tremendously freeing time in the Lord. We have found it so in our lives.

 DISCUSSION

1. How many spiritual gifts did you find?
2. How do you feel about using the whole Bible in developing your understanding of spiritual gifts?
3. Where does LOVE fit in this general study of spiritual gifts? Give a reason for your answer.

 APPLICATION

Share this book with a friend and together make a gifts list. As you make your list discuss your reasons for including or excluding each gift given in chapter 2.

CHAPTER 3

Let's Be Wise

RENEWED INTEREST IN GIFTS

Why are we, or why should we, be interested in the gifts of the Spirit?

There are people who believe spiritual gifts ceased with the apostles or the early church. There are others who are fearful of a discussion on gifts because they have been burned by excesses. There are a growing number of others who don't hold the first position and are aware of the dangers in the second position, but feel we shouldn't as the old saying goes "throw the baby out with the bath water." It is our sincere desire to help those who want to examine the matter of spiritual gifts from a Wesleyan position.

Body Functions as a Unit

We are interested in the gifts of the Spirit, first of all, because it helps the body function as an organic unit. Romans 12:4-5 and 1 Corinthians 12:12-20 clearly teach that the body is made up of many parts yet it functions as a unit. The body is not all a hand or a foot or an eye or an ear. It has all these parts but they work together. Paul states, "So it is with Christ's body" (TLB). There are many different parts, but in Christ we form one body. All the members belong to the others.

In Christ we as the members of the body have different responsibilities. We need different abilities (gifts) so we can do what is needful for the body. Each one has a place to fill, a function to perform, so that the body can function as an organic unit. If we were spiritual amoebas (single-celled animals), we could get along by ourselves. We, in fact, belong to a highly complex body with many members and we need one another. In addition to helping the body function as a unit, the analogy of the church as a body says that all of us are important. Each member is significant.

Growth a Result

Second, a correct understanding of spiritual gifts will help the church to grow. If we know our gift it will cause growth to occur; those who are a part of the body will grow into Christ's likeness (qualitative growth). As we use our gifts others become Christians (quantitative growth). The use of spiritual gifts will cause those within the body to be maturing in Him and those outside the body to be added to Him.

Eliminates Frustration

Third, a good understanding of spiritual gifts will eliminate frustration. An understanding of your gifts will help you find the place where you can most effectively function and serve Christ. You will feel free and happy. Blessing will come to other people.

Suppose that within our physical bodies the liver had

to do the work of the kidneys, or the lungs the work of the heart. Think of all the frustrations these organs would go through, since they are being asked to do something they are not gifted to do. How often within the church we make these demands on people. Suppose you are given the assignment in the church for leadership when your real gift is serving. You will be as frustrated as those you are leading. Or you have been given the place of serving, but your gift is teaching. You likewise will not receive the spiritual blessing you could because you will most likely be frustrated.

One common notion is that service to the Lord should be a bore, difficult, and one certainly should not be happy. This is a false notion. God wants His people to enjoy Him and enjoy serving Him. A good understanding of spiritual gifts will cause both of these things to happen. Spiritual blessings will result, and service to the Lord will be a delight.

Balance to the Body
In the fourth place, an understanding of spiritual gifts will bring balance to the body. Many of our church bodies are misshapen. They remind me of some people I saw in Burundi, when I was a missionary there. As a result of a birth defect or polio, their leg bones and muscles never developed, but they had beautiful, powerful arms. Why? Their arms had to compensate for their lack in their legs. Many members in the body of Christ are not doing their part; as a result, some Christians are very strong, but others are very weak. If each was doing his/her part, there would be balance; the body would not be misshapen.

Gifts are given so that the body can function as a healthy person. Every part in the body has a function to perform and is necessary for the growth and development of that body. In Christ every member has a function to perform, and for every function there is a member.

This has not always been the position of the church. I want to give a brief historical sketch.

HISTORICAL DEVELOPMENT
OF GIFTS IN THE CHURCH

Wesleyans for the first seven decades of the twentieth century skirted around the issue of spiritual gifts. We were leaders in this area of study, but with the rise of the Pentecostal movement in the early 1900s, we dropped our study of this important area in the life of the church. We were fearful of what we perceived as excesses in the areas of prophecy, healing, tongues, and miracles. In the last fifteen years we have once again examined Scripture and are opening ourselves up to what the Lord would say to us about spiritual gifts.

The church has, since the first century, had to contend with excesses that went from ruling gifts out of existence to an over fascination with them.

Heresy and Schism

Following the apostolic era, the church was faced with the problems of heresy and schism. These internal and external threats caused the church to respond by the forming or developing of creeds (statements of correct beliefs), the canon of Scripture (the books considered to be true and of apostolic origin), and by elevating the clergy. In its struggle for existence, little emphasis was placed on the inner workings of the Holy Spirit. As a result, the gifts of the Spirit received little attention by way of careful study. The spiritual life of the church began to sag, and some of the earlier vitality disappeared (Kenneth C. Kinghorn, *Gifts of the Spirit* [Nashville: Abingdon, 1976], pp. 9–19).

In the second century, a group of prophets who relied on the immediate inspiration of the Holy Spirit tried to correct this problem and bring renewal to the church. While we don't want to question the revivalists' vital experience with the Lord, their movement brought serious troubles to the church.

One of the early leaders was Montanus. His movement reacted against the growing secularism in the church. He emphasized the working of the Holy Spirit in the individual without the sermon being delivered or the sacrament being administered. He emphasized a radical separation from the world in preparation for the anticipated imminent return of Christ. While his intentions were pure, he erred in excessive supernaturalism and radical puritanism. Instead of bringing renewal, Montanus divided the church. His movement was labeled schismatic. The leaders of the church became fearful of spiritual excesses with unbridled enthusiasm and fought against it. They preferred order. The church responded by creating the office of priesthood. They elevated the clergy, and made it more difficult for those who desired to enter the priesthood.

A Remarkable Accomplishment

While their efforts to hold tight to order resulted in quenching some of the Holy Spirit's work, the church did a heroic job in those early days. We owe a great debt to their carefulness in establishing orthodoxy, order, and stability. The church grew in spite of great opposition and martyrdom. However, teaching on and use of gifts of the Spirit suffered during this period of time. The elevation of the clergy unfortunately widened a gap between the laity and the priesthood.

The conversion of the Emperor Constantine in A.D. 313 brought new problems to the church; thousands of casual Christians now joined the church. They needed instruction and guidance. The church reacted by further strengthening the concept of the priesthood. People became completely dependent on the clergy for their spiritual welfare and ministry.

Augustine may be considered typical of the church fathers in his attitude toward spiritual gifts. He minimized the working of the Holy Spirit in the individual Christian. His writings, along with others, are vague on the meaning and place of spiritual gifts in the church.

As a result of the great gap between clergy and laity, teaching on the gifts of the Spirit received very little attention. Lay people were not trusted nor given responsibility in the church.

Between the conversion of Constantine in A.D. 313 and the Protestant Reformation in A.D. 1517 the acceptable way for expressing spiritual commitment was to become a monk and enter the monastic movement.

Attempts at Reform

Numerous groups came into existence for expressing this spiritual hunger. Unfortunately, they were unacceptable to the established church and parted ways with it. One such group was the Waldenses, who denounced the abuses of ecclesiastical power and sought to bring renewal of vital Christianity. They emphasized the importance of laymen, rejected prayers to saints, and protested the heavy emphasis on the mass. Along with these possible changes, however, they adopted some non-biblical views. The institutional church saw them as a threat and thus refused to sanction their activities. They, along with other such movements, were either crushed or forced into a noninfluential position. Most of these groups eventually died out.

The monastic movement so emphasized the personal relationship with God that it failed to develop an adequate teaching on the human relational aspects of the Christian faith. As a result of its separation from the world, it did not need to develop a theology of spiritual gifts. Thomas Aquinas, a monk and a theologian of the medieval Roman Catholic Church, drew an equal sign between spiritual gifts and spiritual fruit. Roman Catholicism failed to develop an adequate theology of spiritual gifts.

Protestant Reformers

The Reformers were imprecise in their discussion on gifts. When Luther discussed spiritual gifts he identified them with material blessings or talents. Luther appears to be about as specific as was Thomas Aquinas.

Calvin, in commenting on Romans 12:6-8, referred to ordinary gifts which were to continue perpetually in the church. He failed to clarify what he meant by ordinary gifts. It appears that he was referring to natural talents. He held the view that supernatural gifts ceased with the death of the last apostle. The Reformed tradition, along with some Christian groups, have held that the spiritual gifts were temporary manifestations, experienced only in the days of the apostles.

Wesley and the Methodists

John Wesley and the early Methodists placed their emphasis on the work of the Holy Spirit. Wesley discussed spiritual gifts and believed they were permanent. The church across the ages was to have and use spiritual gifts. Wesley's argument followed this line of thought: the devil still performs false signs and wonders, therefore true signs and wonders must still be in existence.

Wesley believed that gifts are described in two passages, Mark 16:17-18 and 1 Corinthians 12:8-10. In Mark he found five gifts: casting out demons, speaking in new tongues, taking up serpents, drinking any deadly thing, and laying hands on the sick. He denied ever speaking in tongues, taking up serpents, or drinking any deadly thing. In the Corinthian list he found nine gifts: a word of wisdom, a word of knowledge, faith, gifts of healings, miracles, prophecy, discernment of spirits, tongues, and interpretations. Out of this list he claimed only to have the gifts of healings and miracles. He denied he ever laid claim to all of the gifts but does admit to the gifts of exorcism (casting out demons), and of healings and miracles (John Wesley, *The Works of John Wesley* [Grand Rapids: Zondervan, 1872], IX, p. 119).

Wesley did not spend a lot of time defining the gifts or how they should be used. He called some ordinary, others extraordinary. The early Methodists put more emphasis on the excellent way of perfect love.

The Holiness Movement (a movement composed largely of Methodists) became interested in the nature of spiritual gifts during the last part of the nineteenth century.

A Bishop and a Revivalist

Wilson T. Hogue, a bishop in the Free Methodist Church, in his book, *The Holy Spirit, a Study,* has an entire chapter on "The Holy Spirit and His Gifts." He delayed publishing his book for twenty-five years, but wrote most of it between the years 1884–1890. In answering the question, "Were the gifts designated to be permanent?" Bishop Hogue says the traditional answer is no. The extraordinary gifts of the Spirit were to be used only to help get the church established. Once that took place, these gifts were no longer to be considered as belonging to the church. Hogue rejects this answer and states,

Nevertheless, at the risk of being regarded as an enthusiast or a fool, the author is constrained to declare it as his confession of faith regarding this question, that *"the extraordinary gifts of the Holy Ghost, in general, were bequeathed to the whole Church, as a body, and that, too, as a perpetual inheritance"* (Wilson T. Hogue, *The Holy Spirit, a Study* [Chicago: William B. Rose, 1916], pp. 338–39).

Rev. W.B. Godbey, another leader in the Holiness Movement in America, in his book, *Spiritual Gifts and Graces*, published in 1895, devoted half of this small book to a discussion of "the gift and gifts." He saw "the Gift" as the Holy Spirit Himself in sanctifying grace. "The gifts" were given to enable the Christian to conquer Satan and save the world from hell. We are saved by the Gift, but we save others by the gifts.

Godbey states, "A fallen church has hidden these glorious gifts under a bushel the last fifteen hundred years. God has raised up the Holiness people to rescue every item of the long lost Gospel and preach it to the world." He saw it as the Christian's privilege, but also his duty, to receive, appropriate, and utilize all the gifts for the glory of God and the salvation of the world. He concluded his discussion of the gifts by stating that they are free for all and that God commands all to seek them earnestly. No one is at an advantage, since all are on the same level before God. He saw that our efficiency as a Christian soldier did not depend on any physical, educational, or financial advantages nor on the blessing of bishops or ecclesiastical authorities. Our efficiency depended rather on our humble, consecrated, trustful appreciation of these spiritual gifts (W.B. Godbey, *Spiritual Gifts and Graces* [Cincinnati: M.W. Knapp, 1895], pp. 11–12).

These two leaders influenced thousands of people in the Holiness Movement: one as a bishop, the other as a Bible college president.

At the turn of this century a portion of the Pentecostal movement sprang out of the Holiness movement. Pentecostals placed great stress on spiritual gifts. They emphasized two of the gifts: healing and tongues. Many within that tradition believed that physical healing was in the Atonement and that God always wills physical healing. They also insisted that speaking in tongues was a necessary evidence of being filled with the Holy Spirit. Their stress on tongues was so strong the entire Pentecostal phenomenon was known as the "Tongues Movement."

As earlier indicated, for about seven decades in this century many within the Wesleyan and Holiness branches of the church rejected the whole matter of spiritual gifts. They did so because of their fear of excesses. In the last fifteen years our churches are again interested in spiritual gifts.

FACTORS INFLUENCING CHANGE

There are several factors which have brought about this change. The forces which have exerted pressure sprang from a variety of sources. While we will not examine all the sources, it is important to identify some of these factors.

Into the church came a desire to narrow the gap separating laity and clergy. Some wanted to close the gap by declaring all Christians to be ministers. The latter desire has not been achieved, but the former has happened particularly in the independent type churches; some of the traditional churches made significant progress in this area.

Related to this factor has been a new stress on the universal priesthood of believers. All believers have equal access before God.

A third factor has been a renewed interest in the ministry of the Holy Spirit in the believer. The charismatic movement no doubt played a significant part in this interest. One only needs to examine the many recent books published on the Holy Spirit to see that this interest is much broader than the charismatic movement.

Another very important factor has been the emphasis on the church as a body. If the members of the church are part of the body of Christ, how do they relate to one another? Are the members self-sufficient? Or do they need each other as the members of a physical body need each other? The overwhelming answer has been, "We need each other; we can't make it on our own." This factor has caused pastors and thoughtful Christians to reexamine the work of the Holy Spirit in the believer and how that believer relates to the other believers. In other words, once again the church has had to examine the spiritual gifts issue.

DEFINITION OF A SPIRITUAL GIFT

W.T. Purkiser, quoting the Nazarene theologian H. Orton Wiley, says, "The gifts . . . are spiritual endowments for service and are determined by the character of the ministry to be fulfilled" (W.T. Purkiser, *The Gifts of the Spirit* [Kansas City, Missouri: Beacon Hill Press, 1975], p. 19). Kenneth C. Kinghorn of Asbury Theological Seminary says, "A spiritual gift refers to a supernatural enabling of the Holy Spirit which equips a Christian for his work of service and ministry" (Kenneth C. Kinghorn, *Gifts of the Spirit* [Nashville: Abingdon, 1976], p. 20). The definition we are working with in this study is as follows: "A spiritual gift is a unique capacity given by the Holy Spirit to each believer for service/ministry within and to the body of Christ so that it can grow in quality and quantity."

Our definition highlights the common denominators in

most definitions: (1) Gifts are given by the Holy Spirit; (2) they are given to every believer; (3) they are a special enabling given by the Spirit and He determines what each receives; (4) they are given for service and ministry to the body, not just for personal enjoyment.

 DISCUSSION

1. What are four common denominators in the definition of spiritual gifts?
2. In your own words write a definition of spiritual gifts that you could share with a friend.
3. Outline the four reasons given on why we should be interested in spiritual gifts.

 APPLICATION

Before reading chapter 4 make an outline of how spiritual gifts have been used in your life and the life of your church.

Clarifying the Gifts

THE GIFT OF THE SPIRIT

The gift of the Holy Spirit is the Holy Spirit Himself. No other gifts compare to the person of the Holy Spirit dwelling in the believer in His fullness.

Wesleyan churches teach that following the new birth experience believers need to press on in their spiritual quest and be sanctified. God purposes to free the person not only from the penalty for sins but from the power of sin.

In the process of forgiveness the sinner recognizes his/her sins, is convicted of them, repents, and experiences the blood of Jesus; the Holy Spirit witnesses this justification. The person is made new, regenerated by the Holy Spirit, and is adopted into the family of God. This new believer partakes of life in Christ and has the peace and joy of God living within.

However, as nearly all church groups recognize, the person still has a problem with the sinful nature which was inherited from Adam. Theologians call this original sin. Paul in his writings uses many different descriptive terms in depicting this principle active within the believer. He calls it: the sinful nature, the old man, the body of sin, sin that dwells in me, the carnal mind, and the law of sin and death. All churches teach that this too must be removed from the person before he/she can enter a holy heaven and enjoy fellowship with God.

Many believe this is removed from the person just before death or at death; Wesleyans teach that this principle of sin can be cleansed in this life. As the believer recognizes the need and comes to God in full consecration and surrenders, he/she is delivered from this contaminating influence. This is accomplished by cleansing the heart by faith and filling the life with the Holy Spirit.

While the Holy Spirit in His entirety came to the sinner at his adoption into the family of God, the Holy Spirit takes complete possession of the believer in sanctification. The believer can enjoy this grace long before death.

E. Stanley Jones testified to this in his *A Song of Ascents*. "For a year," following his conversion, Jones writes, "I lived under cloudless skies." After this year he found something alien begin to rise in the cellar of his life.

I found there was something down there not in alignment with this new life I had found—ugly tempers, moodiness, deep-down conflicts. The general tenor of life was victory, but there were disturbing intrusions from the depths.

In his search for help, the book *The Christian's Secret of a Happy Life* came into his possession. As he read, God spoke to Jones about giving his all to God. God in turn offered His all, the Holy Spirit, to him. He did just that and life was never the same for him again.

He had been with me, with me in the conscious mind in conversion. Now He was in me, in me in the subconscious. When He was with me in the conscious, it was conversion limited, for the subconscious was not redeemed; cowed and suppressed, but not redeemed. Now the subconscious was redeemed.

God came in the person of the Holy Spirit to fill Jones' life. God both purified his innermost being and gave him power to serve God. Both of these came as a result of his yielding his all to God for His all (E. Stanley Jones, *A Song of Ascents* [Nashville: Abingdon Press, 1968], pp. 51–62).

This coming of the Holy Spirit is the gift of the Spirit spoken about in Acts 2:38; 10:45; 11:17. Peter in commenting on these events in 15:8-9 says, "God, who knows the heart, showed that He accepted them by giving the Holy Spirit to them, just as He did to us. He made no distinction between us and them, for He *purified their hearts by faith*" (emphasis added). It is also the fulfillment of the promises made by John in his preaching, "I baptize you with water, but He will baptize you with the Holy Spirit" (Mark 1:8).

The Holy Spirit is separate from any gifts of the Spirit. The gift of the Holy Spirit is for all believers. Whoever meets the conditions can receive the gift of the Holy Spirit. It is for all believers. All may enjoy this gift or be actively seeking this fullness.

The gifts of the Holy Spirit likewise are for all believers, but God determines what each is to receive. The gifts are given even to immature believers; this happened at Corinth. We believe people can grow in grace, be sanctified, and receive the gift of the Holy Spirit, and the gifts of the Spirit will find their more accurate demonstration.

W.B. Godbey was correct when he wrote, "A popular

heresy on sanctification is to make it the ultimatum on all progress. It is more properly the foundation of a glorious Christian character. . . ." He goes on to say,

> While the gift of the Holy Ghost is the Holy Ghost Himself received as a purifier and abiding comforter in the glorious experience of entire sanctification, the gifts of the Holy Ghost constitute the Christian's [armor] with which he is to conquer Satan and save the world from hell. So we are saved by the gift, but we save others by the gifts (W.B. Godbey, *Spiritual Gifts and Graces* [Cincinnati: M.W. Knapp, 1895], pp. 11–12).

SPIRITUAL FRUIT

The fruit of the Spirit is described in Galatians 5:22-23: Love, joy, peace, patience, kindness, goodness, faithfulness, gentleness, and self-control. In common usage reference is usually made to the *fruits* of the Spirit. The word, however, is in the singular. Some Bible students suggest that the fruit of the Spirit is love. The other eight words are descriptions then of how this love manifests itself. First Corinthians 13 is an excellent commentary on the fruit of the Spirit—love. However one wants to perceive this—whether in the singular or the plural—Scripture teaches that these must be present in the life of the believer.

Every Christian will manifest the fruit of the Spirit. This begins to appear early in the life of the newborn Christian. The fruit will mature and become more plentiful in the life of one who has walked with God for years. If the fruit does not appear in the life of the individual, others are justified in questioning whether the person actually met Jesus. The fruit will be producing Christian character in the person. Fruit really defines what a Christian *is*. Fruit is not discovered but developed through a believer's walk with God. Obedience and yieldedness are the soil, water, and air conditions which cause the fruit to grow and mature.

Gifts help the Christian to know what he/she is to *do* in God's work. They are related to our calling and ministry. They are discovered through service and usage. Each Christian has a gift, but it will differ from what others receive. While the fruit is expected of all believers, there is no one gift that all are expected to receive.

Gifts without fruit are worthless, so states Paul in 1 Corinthians 13. Paul lists several gifts which were held in high esteem by the people (prophecy, languages, faith, poverty, martyrdom), but he says if love is not present, they are all a big inflated zero. Fruit is a prerequisite for the effective use of gifts.

Fruit is everlasting, but gifts are temporary. Faith, hope, and love will abide, but prophecies, languages, knowledge (and the other gifts) will go out of existence. While we are on this earth, God has given us gifts so we might serve Him, that we might accomplish the task He has given us to do. Fruit will abide the eternal fires and will continue to be produced in eternity.

Gifts and fruit are separate. Gifts without fruit will only cause contention and strife. Gifts with fruit will cause the body to function effectively.

NATURAL TALENTS

A question frequently asked by Christians is: "Do my natural talents become my spiritual gifts at conversion?" We need to guard against two extremes. The one extreme is to expect to be zapped with some high-powered gift at some time in one's walk with the Lord. The general expectation is to do something totally out of character. The other extreme is to spiritualize every natural, secular ability a person may have. At a seminar one man suggested that his gift was the gift of gab. The Holy Spirit needs spokespersons but doesn't need idle talk.

All people in this world have natural talents. Most people have several. These natural talents are gifts from God. By these abilities the person can earn a livelihood and serve his fellowman. These abilities help make each person unique. They vary from person to person even among those born to the same parents. These talents need to be discovered and developed. Training can greatly help the person in the use of his/her talents. God gives talents to everyone. He has been generous in that some people, who even refuse to acknowledge His existence, have received many natural abilities. These natural abilities can be used purely for personal enjoyment. Some people become quite egocentric because of their natural talents.

If I were God I'm not sure I'd be as generous as He has been in this area. I'd give more to those who truly follow me and less to those who reject me, but God isn't like that. He gives natural talents to all regardless of their response to Him.

Spiritual gifts are given only to the children of God. They often function through the natural talents, but God is not limited to those expressions. When God gives a gift He doesn't usually give us something that is totally unrelated to our personality. The Christian will dedicate his natural talents to the Lord; God may turn some of them into spiritual gifts. At other times He will give us something that will push us beyond what we might expect.

Loren teaches fifth grade boys at a public school. He earns his living in this way. He enjoys his work and is good at it. He has spent years training, has completed a master's degree and was recently recognized by his school as an outstanding teacher. He uses the natural talents God gave him. Loren believes that teaching has not become his spiritual gift. He knows the mechanics of teaching and from that point of view can do a good job in teaching a class at church. God, for some reason, has not touched this natural talent and turned it into a spiritual gift.

In seminars on spiritual gifts, I have met several teachers who are like Loren. They enjoy their secular work as a teacher but sincerely believe God has not made teaching their spiritual gift. Kathy, on the other hand, is not a trained teacher but God has given her the gift of teaching. She does an excellent job with junior-age girls.

The spiritual gift becomes the individual Christian's contribution to the life of the Christian community of which he/she is a part. These gifts will be employed for the enrichment of the body rather than just personal satisfaction. The Spirit-filled believer who is using the spiritual gift God has given will find tremendous joy and blessing in serving the Lord. He/she will find personal satisfaction and fulfillment; this, however, is not the primary motivation. This person will receive a blessing just as much as he/she will be a blessing. Purkiser has observed, "To be used by God and consciously to cooperate with the Holy Spirit in developing the gifts He gives brings the greatest sense of fulfillment possible to the Christian heart" (W.T. Purkiser, *The Gifts of the Spirit* [Kansas City, Missouri: Beacon Hill Press, 1975], p. 20).

Mark and Diana have musical ability, but when they sing attention is focused on Jesus. Their singing does not cause the hearers to really notice the musicians but rather the One of whom they sing.

Natural talents that have not become spiritual gifts draw attention to the person rather than to the Giver of the gift. A good test as to whether a natural talent has become a spiritual gift is to observe who receives the acclaim—the individual? Or the Savior?

Spiritual gifts will edify and encourage believers. At the same time they will bring conviction to the sinner.

CHRISTIAN ROLES

C. Peter Wagner has helped us in this very important area of study. As you study the Bible, you are struck with certain expectations of all believers.

—We are told that we shall be witnesses (Acts 1:8).
—We are to give (2 Cor. 8–9).
—We are to render wholehearted service (Eph. 6:7).
—We are exhorted to pray (Eph. 6:18).
—We are told that without faith it is impossible to please God (Heb. 11:6).
—We are to practice hospitality (Heb. 13:2).

We could go on. One could imagine that every believer needs every gift if he/she is to meet all of these expectations.

A correct understanding of roles and gifts is helpful here. A role is similar to that of fruit in that it is expected of every Christian. It is related to who we are rather than to what we do. Perhaps this can be shown best by an illustration. When a fire starts, you may not be a fireman, but you do all you can to put the fire out or to get people and things out of the building. You may not be a paramedic, but at the scene of an accident you do all you can to help the injured. Once the experts arrive, firemen and paramedics, you step aside because they are better qualified to deal with the situation.

—All of us are called to be witnesses and on occasion have the joy of leading someone to the Lord. But some have the gift of evangelism and daily have this joy.

—All of us are to have faith but some have the gift of faith and can believe God in situations that look impossible to others.

—All of us are to give to support the Lord's work (the tithe is the beginning), but some go beyond that and don't feel deprived in the least. John Wesley only kept what he felt was essential and gave the rest away.

—All of us are to show hospitality, but some find real joy in serving the Lord in this way.

These are descriptions of our roles as believers. We do them because we are Christians. This does not mean we have a spiritual gift in all the areas.

We need to be careful of gift projection, however. It is easy for the one who has a gift to assume he/she is only doing what all Christians should do and therefore all Christians should do as they do. They fail to recognize their giftedness.

We may not be gifted in a certain area, but when an emergency arises, we exercise our Christian role. Our gift may not be teaching, but if the one who is so gifted becomes ill Saturday evening and the Sunday School superintendent calls us, we gladly accept and exercise our Christian role.

In their service for Christ, people should use their structured time according to their gifts and their unstructured time exercising their roles. Most of us in the church have a limited number of hours to give to the Lord's work. Much of our time is spent earning a living where hopefully we are able to use our natural talents. Some of us are privileged to earn our living by using our spiritual gifts too. The hours people give to the work of God's kingdom should make use of their spiritual gifts. The one with the gift of evangelism should not be saddled down with a lot of committee work, but needs to be released to use his/her time doing evangelism. The one with the gift of teaching should be spending his/her time teaching or preparing for it.

Understanding this distinction has been a very freeing experience for me. God has helped me in leading several people to faith in Christ. However, I do not consider myself to have the gift of evangelism. Before I learned the distinction, I came under a heavy load of guilt. Like Tom I had heard some people testify to leading their seatmates to Christ while on a flight from Los Angeles to Chicago. I have flown some, have tried to be friendly, have taken advantage of opportunities, at least as I perceived them, but have not had the joy of leading anyone to Christ. Only once did I feel I was really able to have a good, deep conversation. For several years I carried this load of guilt, feeling I had somehow failed the Lord. Understanding the distinction between role and gift has freed me up. I still try to be friendly and warm and seek opportunities, but I do not leave a plane with a load of guilt unless I fail to take advantage of an opportunity.

GIFT MIX

How many gifts can a Christian expect to receive? Does each person get only one? Do I get all of the gifts? Scripture is quite clear that every believer has at least one gift (Rom. 12:6; 1 Cor. 12:7; 1 Peter 4:10). "Now to *each one* the manifestation of the Spirit is given for the common good" (1 Cor. 12:7, emphasis added).

God in His grace, graciously gives to each of His children a gift to be used in service and ministry. If Christians are idle in the work of the church, it may be because they have failed to discover and use their spiritual gifts. Some are idle because they are like the one talent person in Matthew 25:14-30 who hid his lord's money. They are not faithful stewards of what God has given them. This is an affront to the Giver and hinders His work here on earth. In many local churches work is not being done because some are failing to discover and use their spiritual gifts. Purkiser has noted,

> The Church at large today is afflicted with a serious unemployment problem: not of people looking for work, but of work looking for people. Wherever this condition is found, both the church and its individual members are impoverished and growth is stunted (W.T. Purkiser, *The Gifts of the Spirit* [Kansas City, Missouri: Beacon Hill Press, 1975], p. 21).

From observation and study it has been found that most people have several gifts — at least two or three. Wagner calls these a gift-mix. These gifts differ according to the calling God has given the person. The pioneer church planter will have more gifts than the pastor of an established church. God seems to give gifts according to the ability and opportunity of the person to exercise them.

Gifts appear to be permanent bestowals. In the gift-mix, the use of one gift may predominate for a period of time because of the nature of the work, and another gift at a later period. Should the original condition return, the former may again predominate.

I believe that part of my gift-mix includes the gifts of teaching and administration. While a missionary in Burundi, I used mainly my gift in administration to give direction to the work of World Gospel Mission. To a lesser extent I used my gift of teaching to train pastors. Since I have been at Western Evangelical Seminary, I have made much greater use of my gift of teaching and to a lesser degree my gift in administration. I believe that should I go back into mission work I would once again make greater use of my gift in administration, and teaching would in most likelihood come in second.

None of the gift passages specifically addresses the issue of the possible loss of spiritual gifts. I have met a few who believe that as a result of carelessness and willful neglect they have lost a spiritual gift. God gave Rebecca the gift of prayer. Following a church split which caused resentment in Rebecca's heart she didn't pray. Rebecca loves the Lord dearly today, and is involved in a good church, but she feels God has taken back the gift He earlier gave to her.

In Scripture we are exhorted to be profitable servants — those who invest and use wisely what has been given to them. We dare not treat lightly what God has so generously given. Knowing what our gifts are and that we will be accountable for the use of these gifts should keep us from wasting our time in nonproductive endeavors. Some people have so many interests that they seem to struggle knowing what they should do, and as a consequence do very little that is of lasting value. It is important for the person to know his/her gifts and give the majority of his/her time in the use of those gifts. This is good stewardship.

In this lesson we have tried to distinguish between the gift of the Spirit and spiritual gifts, spiritual gifts and fruit, natural talents, and Christian roles. We have also noted that all Christians have at least one spiritual gift and that many have several, which we have called their gift-mix.

 DISCUSSION

1. Based on chapter 4, make a chart that gives the similarities and differences between fruit of the Spirit and gifts of the Spirit.

2. Can you explain the difference between gifts and talents?

3. What do you think about gifts and roles?
4. How would you counsel a friend if he/she made these comments?

"Would God give me a spiritual gift in a ministry I enjoyed doing?"

"Can a talent and a gift be the same?"

 APPLICATION

What is more evident in your life—spiritual gifts or fruit of the Spirit?

Are gifts an evidence of spiritual maturity?

For your personal growth, become familiar with three Scripture passages that will be your point of reference on spiritual gifts.

CHAPTER 5

Enabling Gifts

The study of spiritual gifts can be handled in a variety of ways. One way would be to devote a chapter to each gift. This would be very helpful, but would make this book much longer than is intended. Another would be to examine the list in Romans, then Corinthians, then Ephesians, then the other gifts. However one chooses, there is always some arbitrariness to the choice. Recognizing this limitation, we have divided our study of gifts into three categories:

— Enabling Gifts
— Serving Gifts
— Sign Gifts

In Ephesians 4:11-12, Paul gives a list of gifted people after which he says the gifts are given "to prepare God's people for works of service, so that the body of Christ may be built up." The spiritual gifts we will look at in this chapter are primarily gifts which enable other members of the body of Christ to do their work. Kinghorn says the gifts in Ephesians "stand out as higher gifts because they build up the church and prepare the body of Christ for ministry and service" (Kenneth C. Kinghorn, *Gifts of the Spirit* [Nashville: Abingdon, 1976], p. 43). We have added a discussion of missionary, encouragement, wisdom, and knowledge to the gifts of apostleship, prophecy, evangelism, pastor, and teaching found in Ephesians.

APOSTLESHIP

We commonly think of the 12 Apostles of our Lord, those who had been chosen by Him for a very specific purpose, as the apostles. The word *apostle*, however, has a much broader meaning. It means "one who is sent." Frequently, we associate this with our word "missionary."

In Scripture there are people who are referred to as apostles who are not mentioned in the original Twelve (Matt. 10:2-4). Paul, Barnabas, James (the Lord's brother), Silas, and Timothy are all referred to as apostles. There are warnings against false apostles (2 Cor. 11:13; Rev. 2:2). Thus, while the Twelve have a special place among the apostles, there were others. In fact the office of apostleship continues today.

To help us understand the gift of apostleship, we need to examine the work of apostles. These people were sent out by our Lord to preach the Good News of the kingdom, to bring together new groups of believers, and to exercise some authority over them. In contrast to pastors, the apostles take the Gospel to non-Christian peoples and successfully plant the church among them. We can equate this office with the work of the modern-day church planter, particularly with those people who have responsibility for several such churches. The apostle is a person who has many of the gifts of the Spirit because of the heavy demands that are placed on him. The new Christians look to him for everything they know about Christianity. In order to adequately fulfill the gift, apostles also need leadership, faith, evangelism, teaching, and pastoring gifts. The church needs many more apostles if it is ever to make the impact that is necessary in today's unevangelized world.

I met Robert Johnson of Salem, Oregon, a retired pastor. Across twenty-five years of church planting (1950–1975), he brought into existence twenty-eight churches. When I interviewed him in 1986, all but six of those were still worshiping congregations. In my mind he fits the mold of an apostle. He planted churches among his own people. He did not need to learn another language or culture in order to do his work. The average time period for a church to be fully organized under Robert Johnson's ministry was eleven months. One church was organized in thirty days.

PROPHECY

There is a modern notion when one hears the word "prophet," that the speaker will tell you something about the future, something that is not presently known. While prophets in Scripture did make some predictions, their prophecies dealt mainly with the present; they illustrated them from the past. Prophecy has more to do with "forth-telling" than "fore-telling."

It implies the declaration of the Word of God with divine anointing and empowering. It is the kind of proclamation that produces divine conviction within the hearts of those who hear. Peter on the Day of Pentecost, when he quoted Joel 2:28-32, seemed to have this definition in mind. Following this proclamation, the result was divine conviction for sin (Acts 2:37). Agabus in Acts made a couple of predictions that came true, but most of the prophets made God's Word relevant to the immediate situation.

Kinghorn states, "Prophecy fundamentally means light for the present" (Kenneth C. Kinghorn, *Gifts of the Spirit* [Nashville: Abingdon, 1976], p. 49). Bishop Hogue would be in agreement with this when he wrote, "To prophesy, in the general New Testament sense of the term, is to teach or expound the Scriptures, or to impart spiritual instruction, under the extraordinary power and illumination of the Holy Spirit" (Wilson T. Hogue, *The Holy Spirit, a Study* [Chicago: William B. Rose, 1916], p. 333).

True prophecy (1 Cor. 14) will edify and build up the believers, encourage and impart life, console the people of God, and bring conviction to the sinner. It is the one gift Paul encouraged the people to seek and must be considered the higher gift. God gives it to lay people as well as clergy. There also is no sex distinction. Philip's daughters were prophets within the early church.

Prophecy is needful today. It is one of God's most common ways to bring people face-to-face with His truth. The one effectively using this gift encourages people to respond to the living Lord. It imparts new inspiration and illumination to the Word. The prophet prepares him/herself through the careful study of the Word. God's Spirit then sets on fire what His servant has taken in.

In Scripture the prophet coupled his declaration of the Word of the Lord with warnings. If the people failed to heed the Word of the Lord spoken through the prophet, judgment would follow. Jonah is a good example of a prophet to Gentile peoples. Hosea is an example of a prophet who called the people of Israel to repentance.

Prophets are usually unpopular with the people. Pastors and evangelists are modern prophets when they denounce sin and call people to obedience to the Word of God. If all people speak well of the leader, that leader may need to examine whether he/she is declaring all that is in the Word of God.

EVANGELISM

Evangelism means primarily to share good news. Frequently we caricaturize the evangelist as one who, with Bible uplifted in one hand, pounds the pulpit with the other and hurls out the divine thunderbolts of wrath and judgment. While this has its place, another image may be more helpful. It is that of one beggar telling another where he found bread. It is the sharing of Good News.

All Christians are to be witnesses (Acts 1:8). We are to share our faith in Christ and to take advantage of the opportunities that come our way to point others to the Living Fountain. Some people though have a special ability to lead many others to faith in Christ. They can speak to unconverted people, and God gives them remarkable success in seeing these people accept God's offer of salvation. These people are like spiritual midwives. They can sense when a person is really ready to hear and accept the Gospel message. They know just the right thing to say or do. The fruit is ripe and all they do is pick it.

Frequently, these people do not recognize their ability to win souls as a gift, but think they are only exercising their Christian role of witnessing. Others without this gift may come under a heavy cloud of guilt when they don't experience the same results. Those without the gift of evangelism need to learn from those with it, so they can more effectively witness. All of us need to be more aware of opportunities as they come.

C. Peter Wagner has estimated that about 10 percent of Christians have the gift of evangelism. He has studied evangelism programs in several churches and has found that about 10 percent of the people are involved and are effective. Studies I have conducted in conjunction with spiritual gifts seminars indicate that 10 percent is too high of a percentage. Regardless of the percentage, the most productive people in a church from an evangelism point of view are those with the gift for evangelism and the new converts. The new converts have the most natural bridges back to people still in the world. Blessed is the congregation who takes advantage of these two groups within their body.

PASTOR

The gift of pastor could also be called that of a shepherd. Kinghorn says, "The terms 'bishop,' 'elder,' and 'shepherd' are synonyms in the New Testament. Shepherd refers to what one does; overseer [or bishop] refers to how one does it; and elder refers to the place the shepherd has in the Christian community" (Kenneth C. Kinghorn, *Gifts of the Spirit* [Nashville: Abingdon, 1976], p. 54).

The one with the gift of pastor assumes responsibility for the spiritual welfare of a group of people. He or she feeds them, guides them, and ministers to them much as a shepherd does. To help us understand the concept, keep in mind the Eastern model of a shepherd who is with his flock day and night. Our American model of sheep in a fenced-in-lot left to themselves does not fit.

A good shepherd protects his/her flock from evil and leads them into good pastures. The shepherd is not only concerned for the physical well-being of the flock, he/she is concerned for the spiritual well-being. To this end, the shepherd calls on the flock, spends time with them, and really gets to know them. The pastor does not dictate to or drive his flock, but rather leads them and provides for them.

Frequently, we associate the gift of pastor with the one who has the office of pastor. Implied in this is the feeling that pastoring is a clergy-type gift. But many lay people possess the gift of pastor. The Sunday School teacher who is concerned for the class, seeks them out when they miss, prays for them, counsels them, and is concerned for their spiritual welfare, is exercising the gift of pastor. The same could be said for the youth director who has this same concern for the young people; the choir director who carries this concern for the choir; the Bible study leader who likewise shows this concern for those in the Bible study group. All are exercising the gift of pastor.

The person holding the office of pastor will recognize the need for these undershepherds. As a body of believers grows, the pastor will spend more of his/her time with the undershepherds, enabling them to exercise their gifts so that the flock of God is truly pastored. In the natural world, the shepherd has to spend more time with the sheep when they are lambing, so the spiritual shepherd will spend more time with the newborn lambs in God's great flock. They will need more of his/her attention than those who have walked with God for a number of years.

TEACHING

Those with the gift of teaching make truths of the Christian faith live for others. The truth is understood and applied to life. It is not the repetition of dull facts, but the impartation of living truths within the life of the individual. The one with the gift of teaching is able to bring clarity to things difficult to understand and unity to what at first appears to be unrelated facts or events. In this way the student receives help, insight, and understanding. The end result is edification.

A good teacher is both content- and learner-oriented. To stress content alone tends to be unrelated to the student's life. To stress the learner's present situation only tends toward superficiality. The good teacher brings the two together in an exciting and relevant manner.

The church has great need for teaching. People need to develop a good understanding of Scripture and the truths it contains. Without this, the body of believers will remain immature in Christ. They will never put their roots down and be able to stand the winds that will blow against them.

Our American culture is taken up with instants — instant mashed potatoes, instant dinners, instant success. We tend to want instant religion too. While it is true that we receive Christ at an instant in time and the Holy Spirit fills our hearts in an instant, this is just the beginning. There must follow the whole growth process — the maturing process. This is more like the growing of an oak than a Christmas tree. Good teaching is part of the process. It is recorded in Acts 2:42, "They devoted themselves to the apostles' teaching." Teaching and those with the gift of teaching are urgently needed in the church.

MISSIONARY

The gift of the missionary, while not directly mentioned in a gift list in Scripture, nevertheless was used in the New Testament. Paul obviously had it, while Peter did not. As was mentioned in our study of "apostle," its root meaning is "a sent one." This fits our common understanding for the word "missionary," someone sent from one church to minister to a different group of people. As we went on to define the gift of apostleship, we found that this person was responsible for preaching Christ where He was not known and for bringing into existence a group(s) of believers. This takes place among the people from whom the apostle originated, as was true of Robert Johnson. The one exercising this gift does not need to learn another language, culture, or cross any other significant barrier except the sin barrier in order to do his/her work. Peter was quite effective in this type of work.

The one with the gift of missionary is able to minister his/her other spiritual gifts in a cross-cultural situation. They can do this with ease and comfort. Paul was much more effective in this area than Peter. The missionary who also has the gift of apostleship would be a cross-cultural church planter. We need many of this type. The missionary with the gift of evangelism would be effective in leading people outside his own culture to faith in Christ; the teacher would make the truths of God's Word alive and impactful for the people in the other culture.

C. Peter Wagner suggests that the one with the gift of missionary enjoys coming into contact with people of another culture. If they get culture shock, they get over it more quickly than others. They become immune to the new bugs in the food and drink. They learn the language more quickly. They pick up on slang words, body language, and tone of voice not described in textbooks. They feel at home with people from a second culture and are eventually accepted as "one of us." When gone from their people they can hardly wait to get back (C. Peter Wagner, *Your Spiritual Gifts Can Help Your Church Grow* [Glendale, California: Regal, 1974], p. 204–6).

All missionaries go through cultural adjustments; most experience culture shock. During this period, things back home take on special significance: a piece of apple pie, a McDonald's hamburger, a cup of coffee at the favorite restaurant. The things of the host country are generally despised. The one with the gift of missionary soon learns to enjoy and love the rice and beans, the papaya and star fruit, the strong, sweet tea or coffee. They begin to miss these things when they are in their home culture and can hardly wait to get back to their people.

Harold and Hettie Shingledecker went to Burundi as missionaries in 1944. Since World War II was still in progress they had to go to Argentina and book passage across the South Atlantic. After arriving in South Africa, they traveled by train and boat to get to Burundi. For the next thirty-five years they planted churches, taught classes for the new pastors, printed songbooks and tracts, and did all the other things missionaries need to do. They raised four children in Burundi, all of whom are missionaries today. Harold and Hettie left Burundi in 1979 to begin retirement. They loved the people of Burundi and were loved by them. I believe both have the missionary gift.

The church needs an increasing number of people with the gift of missionary. There are 3 billion people in the world today who, if they are reached with the Gospel, will be reached by those who have the missionary gift. There is no one who knows their language and culture sufficiently that they can hear the message without someone going this extra distance.

ENCOURAGEMENT (EXHORTATION)

Those who possess this gift may not be as aware of it as those who have the other gifts we have mentioned. People around them, however, are aware of it. Barnabas is perhaps our best scriptural example in regard to this gift. His name means "son of encouragement" (Acts 4:36). The one possessing this gift is equipped for a ministry of calling forth the best in others. "The function of this spiritual gift is to lift up, encourage, strengthen, and admonish another to become his best self in Christ" (Kenneth C. Kinghorn, *Gifts of the Spirit* [Nashville: Abingdon, 1976], p. 88). This word in Greek comes from the same root as paraclete or "comforter." It has the idea of "going to another person's help" (W.T. Purkiser, *The Gifts of the Spirit* [Kansas City, Missouri: Beacon Hill Press, 1975], p. 30).

This gift does not suggest the idea of berating other people for their sins or of shaming them. It seeks rather to lift them higher than they are. It is generally used in private conversation, though on occasion it may be exercised in a public way. The one with this gift generally comes along in just the right time to pick us up and help us in our pilgrimage with Christ. We may be discouraged and they cheer us up. We may need a word of correction and they give it. In today's hurting world, we need more people with the gift of encouragement.

When I was a young missionary in Burundi, one of my senior colleagues did just this for me. Bill Cox, at just the opportune time, would come up to me and say, "I'm sure glad you're here," or, "I sure appreciate you." He didn't always know the struggles I was going through, as I tend to keep things in rather than let them out, but what encouragement I drew from those few words. A word of support, of counsel, even an occasional word of rebuke can really strengthen our fellow travelers on their pilgrimage to the heavenly city.

WISDOM

Wisdom and knowledge go together, but in order to bring clarity we will look at each one separately. There are promises in God's Word that He will give wisdom to those who lack (James 1:5). There are examples of those who had great wisdom and could answer in this way. Jesus on several occasions confounded His adversaries (Luke 13:7; 14:6; 20:40). Paul said that when he came to Corinth, he spoke with a wisdom given by God (1 Cor. 2:6-10, 14-16). Stephen at his trial, likewise, had the gift of wisdom (Acts 6:10).

The gift of wisdom is the right use of knowledge. The one with it can apply God's truth to a problem or need that is facing the body. As Jesus promised the disciples that they would be given wisdom to answer when on trial (Luke 21:14-15), so the one with this gift receives divine insight for the specific situations facing the church.

Godbey and Hogue both understood this gift to apply to divine insight when presenting the Gospel to the unconverted. The Christian may be confronted with a situation that is totally new to him. God gives him divine wisdom as to how to proceed so that these people come to faith in Christ. Kinghorn expands on this and suggests that anointed speaking and writing will regularly incorporate this gift. "It is through this gift that God enables one to communicate his truth in such a way that it penetrates effectively into the hearts of other people" (Kenneth C. Kinghorn, *Gifts of the Spirit* [Nashville: Abingdon, 1976], p. 62).

In the West we equate education with schooling and call a person well educated if he has completed several years of graduate study. Many of my African brothers had little opportunity for formal schooling, but they were highly educated people. I was constantly amazed at the insights and wisdom they would bring to a situation. Some of this was natural for them, but some was definitely a gift from God.

Many lay people have this gift. The one with this gift can take diverse facts and arrange them in an order that makes sense to the others.

KNOWLEDGE

Knowledge has to do with comprehension of facts, recognition of truth, or a coming to know. How does one come to know? In the natural world, the scholar, the research specialist, and others must have the natural talent to handle "tons" of information. They need to keep their facts straight and know the truths of their discipline of study or work.

In the spiritual realm there is need for those with the gift of knowledge. This enables them to bring divine insight to the Scriptures. These people will be good with the details of Scripture, of archeology, and/or the fine shades of meaning in the biblical languages. Some of this they have gathered through diligent study, but some of it comes as a gift from the Spirit. The ones with this gift will be drawn to give themselves in study.

There are others who may not have had the opportunity for extended study yet to whom have been revealed insights into God's Word by their encounter with the living Lord (1 Cor. 2:10-16). In Paul's case, he had studied, but his mind and heart had been closed to God's truth. Once his heart was open, God gave him great insight into the mysteries of God.

In comparing and contrasting knowledge and wisdom, knowledge has more to do with facts, data, insight. Wisdom then makes wise use of that body of knowledge in meeting a particular need or situation.

In this study of enabling gifts, we have looked at: apostleship, prophecy, evangelism, pastor, teaching, missionary, encouragement, wisdom, and knowledge. God has gifted some within the body with these gifts. Because many who have these gifts are up-front, easily observed by others, we tend to think they are more important. The service gifts and sign gifts are equally important, and in the next two chapters we will see why.

 DISCUSSION

1. Of the nine equipping gifts, which are you the most familiar with?
2. Could you identify two specific qualities that would be true of all the equipping gifts?

3. How would you explain these two qualities to a friend?

 APPLICATION

During the coming week see how many of the enabling gifts are functioning in your church.

Do you think you might have one of these gifts?

CHAPTER 6

Serving Gifts

I n our body it is easy to see the hands, feet, eyes, ears, and nose. There are other members of our body that we never see, such as, the heart, lungs, and liver. These are covered up and are not for public display.

Some gifts in the body of Christ as like our external organs. We see those who exercise these gifts. Among them would be the evangelist, the pastor, the missionary. There are other gifts in the body of Christ that are like our internal organs; we seldom see them. They are the intercessors, the ones showing hospitality, the ones showing mercy. It is these serving gifts we want to examine in this lesson. We want to remind you that all of these gifts are needed; all are important. We can't get along without each other.

HELPS

The gifts of helps and service are closely related gifts. The Greek word for helps in 1 Corinthians 12:28 means being a support or help to those in need. The gift of service (Rom. 12:7) comes from the Greek word for deacon which means "one who serves." We are not seeking to draw a sharp line of distinction between these two gifts, only to point out some shades of distinction.

People with the gift of helps tend to a person-centered ministry. Their spiritual gift is to help others, often in a one-to-one situation. Few of us have ever heard of these women: Leola Linkous, Stephanie Wills, Marge Kelley, and Irma Griswold. They are the secretaries or administrative assistants for these well-known people: Leighton Ford, Billy Graham, Robert Schuller, and Bill Bright. The effectiveness of these men would be greatly reduced without the able assistance these women render (C. Peter Wagner, *Your Spiritual Gifts Can Help Your Church Grow* [Glendale, California: Regal, 1974], pp. 224–25).

Persons with the gift of helps are often behind the scenes helping to release other workers in their spiritual ministries. They do so in such a way that it strengthens and encourages those they help.

Many lay people possess this gift. They strengthen the hands of those they serve. They are like Aaron and Hur who held up the hands of Moses (Ex. 17:10-12). They free those they serve from some of the administrative tasks so they can give themselves to the ministry God has called them to. Those with the gift of helps find spiritual fulfillment in assisting others.

SERVICE

Service, instead of being a person-centered ministry, equips one for task-centered ministries. These people are aware of the needs of a body of believers. Their gift enables them to meet the physical and material needs of others in a gracious manner.

The deacons in Acts 6 are a good example of the gift of serving. The church faced its most serious internal challenge. Greek-speaking widows were neglected in favor of the Hebrew-speaking widows. The church selected the seven deacons to rectify the problem. They used the resources which were available and found a solution that was best for all concerned. This ministry by the deacons relieved the apostles for their calling. It also met the needs of the widows among the Greek-speaking Jews.

Some organizations within the church have dedicated themselves to this type of ministry. Many men's and women's groups make themselves responsible to supply items of equipment for missionaries so they can do their work more effectively. Those who find their spiritual satisfaction in supplying these needs have the gift of service.

In my missionary work, we used a lot of eucalyptus poles to build churches. The trees could be cut with axes and saws, but it took many days to do all the work that was necessary to build a church. A man in Oregon, Ed Albee, who worked for a chain saw manufacturing corporation, felt compelled to provide me with the saw, several chains, and repair parts. He perceived a need, believed he and others could meet that need, and did it. What an asset that piece of equipment was to me and the African church leaders. We could frame a church in just a day or two depending on the size and on the distance we had to haul the poles.

MERCY

Those who have the gift of mercy are certainly among the least-sung about workers in Christ's great body. They are very important; one cannot exaggerate their value. One college professor has estimated that if 95 percent of all the books and pamphlets written, lectures delivered, and learned papers read were never written or were lost, we wouldn't lose all that much. What really counts in life is our interpersonal relationships—the way we treat our spouses, our children, our neighbors, our fellow travelers along the pilgrimage of life. The acts of kindness and concern are what really make an impact on the lives of people.

The gift of mercy or compassion is more than just pity for someone; it is real empathy. It is a sensitivity to the feelings of others. It is an ability "to walk in their moccasins." The gift enables one to feel with those in need. Yet, it goes beyond feeling to action. When there is sickness or a death in the family, dishes of food are brought in to help alleviate hunger. The house may be cleaned or the clothes washed for the person who is too ill to do this routine work.

There is a great army of such people who minister to those who have physical, mental, and emotional handicaps. There are some who minister to those who are shut in. Others minister to the poor and underprivileged, and others to the alcoholics and prostitutes. They visit those in the nursing homes; they take birthday cakes to help them celebrate their birthdays. God has gifted these people with compassion for those who suffer misfortune in life.

They do not render this service grudgingly; they do it cheerfully. They tend to see good motives in those served even when their expression of it may be less than acceptable. Blessing comes to those ministered to; but the ones ministering also receive a blessing. These people are the ones who give a cup of cold water in Jesus' name. Service is rendered both to believers and to unbelievers.

Jack and Arlene Seeley ministered in Seattle's inner city and sought to assist the homeless, abused women, and others in need. They received few commendations from those they served; sometimes the street people even made it difficult for the Seeleys. Day by day and week by week, they extended God's mercy to them. They did this cheerfully and without reserve.

HOSPITALITY

Peter adds this gift to our study (1 Peter 4:9-10): "Offer hospitality to one another without grumbling. Each one should use whatever gift he has received to serve others, faithfully administering God's grace in its various forms." There are other exhortations in Scripture to be hospitable: Romans 12:13; Titus 1:8; 1 Timothy 3:2; Hebrews 13:2.

Hospitality really refers to the love of strangers. The ones with this gift provide an open house and a warm welcome to the visitor. With the multiplication of motels and restaurants across America, we seldom are asked to entertain a traveler such as was true in ancient times. In many parts of the world, the only place to stay if you are traveling, is in the home of someone who lives where you happen to be at the close of the day.

I learned much from the Africans in this regard when I was in Burundi. Anyone needing lodging for the evening was given it. If they arrived at mealtime, they shared what they had even though it meant that each family member would have a smaller portion.

This gift is still manifest in America by inviting visitors in church home for Sunday dinner. It is also manifest in providing a room and meals for traveling Christian workers whether they be missionaries, evangelists, pastors, or professors.

Those with this gift recognize that the warmth and love in the home is more important than using the best china, silver, and tablecloth on the table. It is possible to serve smaller than normal portions and not offend the guest. What the guest will remember is the true hospitality rather than the food or the table service.

The demand for this gift may not be as high in America as in Africa, but there are sanctified believers who exercise this gift and God's kingdom is advanced as a result of it.

GIVING

Several years ago when Billy Graham was holding a crusade in Madison Square Garden, a well-known underworld character walked in along with four bodyguards. At the offering time the guards looked to their boss to see what to do. He told them, "This one is on me." He then pulled from his pocket a wad of $100 bills. "The wad was thick enough to choke a cow" or so it was reported by those sitting behind the man. The underworld character went through these $100 bills until he came to a $1 bill which he put in the plate (Leslie B. Flynn, *19 Gifts of the Spirit* [Wheaton, Illinois: Victor Books, 1981], pp. 118–19).

This man did not have the gift of giving nor was he fulfilling the role of a Christian to tithe. When we discussed the distinction between gift and role, we suggested that the role of giving for all Christians is the tithe. Those who tithe are simply doing their Christian duty. People do cheat the IRS and get away with it. We can't cheat on God and get away with it. C. Peter Wagner attends an upper middle-class church in Southern California. One time he figured that if all the people in that church were living on welfare payments and tithed, the church's income would increase by 40 percent.

The one with the gift of giving not only gives the tithe, but beyond this. God enables them to understand the material needs of others and to then meet those needs, doing so generously. Frequently, they find that as they give, they answer the prayers of the other person down to the very dollar amount.

Glaphré tells of people who met her needs. She had prepared a notebook for her *Prayerlife* ministry.

> After I had written the notebooks for the adult seminar, I learned that the initial printing costs totaled $1,000. I waited. While in Florida, I received a long-distance phone call from a couple in Oklahoma, who felt impressed to give $1,000 to Prayerlife.
> One thousand dollars! I could hardly believe it. That was so much more than I'd ever received before. And without anyone at all knowing the need, the exact amount had been given. I ordered the first small shipment of notebooks (Glaphré, *When the Pieces Don't Fit . . . God Makes the Difference* [Grand Rapids: Zondervan, 1984], p. 130).

Often these people forego certain rights or privileges they could enjoy so that the cause of Christ can be advanced. To others they appear frugal because they do not spend more than is necessary on themselves. They often give anonymously, so that their gift goes unnoticed.

The gift of giving involves giving freely, liberally, with delight so that God's work will be advanced. They receive spiritual blessing in giving in this way. These are not always wealthy people, just ordinary people with ordinary incomes who love to give.

John Wesley went beyond just this gift of giving to what we could call voluntary poverty. Instead of living more lavishly as his salary increased, he gave it away. He denied himself beyond what many do.

FAITH

If we are Christians we must have faith. We believe that God exists. We must believe that God hears us when we pray. We must believe that He forgives our sins when we confess them to Him in sincere repentance. We also believe that He sanctifies our hearts when we yield ourselves to Him. By faith, we believe God goes with us day by day, leading us as we walk with Him. This refers to what we have called the role of faith. It could also be called the grace of faith. When we become Christians we live at this level.

There are some with the gift of faith. Faith-gifted people, in a special way, are able to believe that God is adequate for a certain situation and to tap His resources. These people have an extraordinary confidence in God's ability to meet the need. Kinghorn says they go beyond a mere affirmation of God's promises. "The gift of faith takes hold of biblical principles, and under the inspiration of the Holy Spirit applies them to the current situation. The gift of faith enables one to believe God for mighty results" (Kenneth C. Kinghorn, *Gifts of the Spirit* [Nashville: Abingdon, 1976], p. 66).

Godbey understood this gift to be the instrument "in the conviction, conversion and sanctification of others." He cited several examples of people, among them housewives and the ill, who were able to pray the prayer of faith for revival for a certain church or people (W.B. Godbey, *Spiritual Gifts and Graces* [Cincinnati: M.W. Knapp, 1895], p. 20).

James Hudson Taylor began praying for 100 new missionaries for China, and before the year was up 102 had actually left for China. He was as confident that this would happen at the beginning of the year before even one had left England, as he was at the end of the year when it actually happened.

Those with the gift of faith believe God will do miracles in the face of natural impossibilities and He will accomplish this by divine intervention.

PRAYER

This gift is part B of faith. Prayer and faith go together. Whoever has the gift of faith spends time in prayer. The one who prays must have faith in God to do what is prayed for. As with faith, every Christian is expected to pray. We thank the Lord for our daily food. We seek Him for His direction in our lives. We pray for things that concern us. We pray in private and in public. What we have been describing is part of the role of being a Christian. Because we have received the grace of God, we follow the example of our Lord who spent time in prayer.

How long should a Christian pray? Probably longer than most of us do. I once read that the average minister spends seven minutes a day in prayer. If that is true, how long does the average layperson spend? Most of us could spend more time in prayer and still not overdo it.

Those with the gift of faith and prayer frequently spend prolonged periods in prayer. When they are through, it seems as if only a few moments have gone by.

George Müller, who opened several orphanages in England, was a man known for his faith and prayer. Flynn, in *19 Gifts of the Spirit*, reports a case when fog was hindering Müller from keeping an engagement.

A trans-Atlantic sea captain, after 22 hours on the ship's bridge in a dense fog off the banks of Newfoundland, was startled by a tap on the shoulder. It was Müller, then in his 70s. "Captain, I have come to tell you I must be in Quebec on Saturday afternoon." This was Wednesday.

When the captain said it was impossible, Müller replied, "If your boat can't take me, God will find some other way. I've never broken an engagement in 57 years."

"I'd like to help," responded the captain, "but what can I do?"

"Let's go below and pray," Müller suggested.

"But Mr. Müller, don't you know how dense the fog is?"

"My eye is not on the fog, but on God who controls the fog and every circumstance of my life."

Down on his knees, Müller prayed the simplest prayer the captain had ever heard. In his opinion it fit a child of nine. "O Lord, if Thou wilt, remove this fog in five minutes. Thou dost know the engagement made for me in Quebec for Saturday."

Putting his hand on the captain's shoulder, Müller restrained him from praying. "First, you don't believe God will do it, and second, I believe He has done it, so there's no need for you to pray. Open the door, Captain, and you'll find the fog gone." And so it was. Müller kept his Saturday engagement in Quebec.

Modestly, Müller wrote, "It pleased the Lord to give me in some cases something like the gift of faith, so that unconditionally I could ask and look for an answer" (Leslie B. Flynn, *19 Gifts of the Spirit* [Wheaton, Illinois: Victor Books, 1981], pp. 142–43).

Many older people receive this gift. They can't be as active as they once were because of physical limitation. They take prayer requests seriously and pray until the answer comes. We need many more people who will seek this gift and will give themselves to it.

LEADERSHIP

The gift of leadership and the gift of administration are assumed to go together. They do so in some people, but not in others. We have separated them for closer observation.

People with the gift of leadership are often the idea people. They see where the group should go or what they should do. Their vision and style engender confidence in others to follow them. In the area of missions Dr. Ralph Winter is an example of an idea person. He is constantly challenging mission leaders with new possibilities.

The ones with the gift of leadership have the ability to preside, govern, and plan with wisdom, fairness, example, humility, confidence, ease, and efficiency. They do not manipulate people or coerce them; rather, people follow. They are not bosses, but servants. The Bible uses various terms to speak of leaders. It calls them elders (Acts 20:17), bishops, and deacons (Phil. 1:1). There are descriptive lists for leaders in Titus 1 and 1 Timothy 3.

In a local church, the pastor should be the one who provides the general leadership for that local body. Others within the congregation are leaders as well. Blessed is the pastor, if he/she is not the chairperson, who has a chairperson of the Board who is a leader rather than a follower.

ADMINISTRATION

Administrators, in contrast to the leaders and idea people, are the doers. They know how to put into effect the ideas the leaders have developed. To use a common expression, they tend to be the nuts and bolts people. Administrators have an amazing ability to bring into being what the leaders have conceived, and once it has been brought into being, to see that it continues to operate in a smooth way.

These people can organize and administer. They too do it with wisdom, fairness, humility, confidence, ease, and efficiency. They enjoy long hours in the office, overseeing the business matters, keeping everything running smoothly. They receive spiritual delight from keeping the Sunday School operating well. They help keep the records and see that the program the C.E. Department has envisaged is on target and running smoothly.

DISCERNMENT OF SPIRITS

John wrote to the believers in 1 John 4:1, "Dear friends, do not believe every spirit, but test the spirits to see whether they are from God, because many false prophets have gone out into the world." This is part of the role expectation of every Christian. God gives some a special gift so they can quickly discern if a spirit is the Holy Spirit, a human spirit, or a demonic spirit. The one with this gift can discern correct, true teaching from false and misleading teaching. This is not necessarily the ability to tell whether someone else is a believer, however.

Paul tells us that Satan disguises himself as a servant of light (2 Cor. 11:14-15). It is not surprising that some of his servants know all the right words to say and make it sound quite plausible when in reality their teaching comes from the pit. The one with discernment will be able to determine this false teaching.

The one with discernment can detect when the spirit is only that of the human spirit. Unfortunately, there are things accredited to the Holy Spirit which are only whipped-up human enthusiasm, much as in a high school pep rally. A "Hallelujah" or an "Amen" can truly be spoken under the anointing of the Holy Spirit. In cases where it is encouraged excessively from the platform or from the leader, it can be purely the human spirit reacting.

There are times when things become dead because they are only routine and God must do something new to breathe life into the situation. The one with discernment will detect that this new thing is truly the work of God and will encourage this new expression.

Discernment will also help the individual know where a congregation is spiritually so he/she will minister to them in the manner that is most needful. There is little use in preaching sanctification to people who have never been converted. If people are being obedient to what God is telling them, they need to be fed instead of only being told to be converted or to be sanctified.

CRAFTSMANSHIP

As has been noted, this gift is not in any New Testament list. Oholiab was a skilled craftsman. God said, "I have put that skill in him" (Ex. 31:3-11, author's paraphrase).

The ones with this gift like to work with their hands. They can take a chunk of stone and create a beautiful statue, a piece of wood and turn it into a beautiful Communion table, or flowers and arrange them in a way others enjoy. Some plant the flowers and make the churchyard beautiful. Others take flour, sugar, eggs, and other ingredients and create a beautiful cake or a pan of rolls. Still others take a broken item most would throw out and restore it to usefulness and service. Some can take paints, a brush, and a canvas and create a beautiful picture that blesses the hearts of men and lifts their souls heavenward. Frequently these people find it very hard to be up-front. If they had to speak for five minutes in a public service, they would rather die.

MUSIC

Music is another gift not specifically mentioned in a New Testament gifts list. Music is mentioned in the New Testament (1 Cor. 14:26; Eph. 5:19-20; Col. 3:16).

God has gifted certain people to be able to either sing or play an instrument so that others are helped in their walk with the Lord. David, the King of Israel, was one who was gifted in the ability to write music, play an instrument, and sing. Many of his songs have come down to us in the Book of Psalms.

Those who have this as a spiritual gift are able to bless the hearts of the believers; edification is the result. Sinners are likewise convicted and drawn to the Savior. Troubled hearts are quieted before the Creator of the universe through music and songs. God wants to pour out blessing on many through the use of their gift of music.

Music can be natural talent only. If they become spiritual gifts, they point people to Jesus. Attention is drawn to Him rather than to the musician or the craftsman.

The serving gifts generally are "behind the scenes" types of gifts. Often these people do not receive much attention except when they are missing. Then their gifts are recognized by all because they are missing. They are like the voice box that has been injured or has laryngitis.

 DISCUSSION

1. Using the information in chapter 6 make a chart listing the twelve serving gifts. (On this chart give a short definition, an area of ministry, and how the gift may be used in that area of ministry.)

2. Do you think people with serving gifts need training? (List the type of training you think would be appropriate.)

 APPLICATION

The next time you are in church, make a list of the serving gifts you see working. Now match names of people with that list.

CHAPTER 7

Sign Gifts

S ign gifts when properly used have been like signs that attract people to Jesus. In many mission lands, miracles, divine healing, and exorcism have been convincing proofs to the people that there is power in the Gospel. They have seen it demonstrated, and they are willing to put their trust in God as a result of the sign. We may debate whether this is good or bad. "If a sign gets them, a sign will lose them." While this is true, nevertheless God has used signs and wonders in many places.

Sign gifts are also more sensational than the other gifts. They call more attention to themselves. These gifts have been more abused than the other gifts. No doubt Satan has imitated these gifts at certain times and has misled people into false movements. Just because this has happened does not mean we should rule them out of existence, but should develop a correct understanding of them. We believe these gifts have caused more heated discussions as well as division within the church than all the other gifts combined.

So while we are warning the reader that there is some troubled water ahead, we are not suggesting the reader should abandon his/her trip at this point.

MIRACLES

Evangelical Christians believe in miracles in the New Testament. We read of miracles that Jesus performed. He turned water to wine. Peter was able to walk on water. Jesus fed 5,000 people with five loaves and two fish, and He raised dead people to life again. We also read of the miracles performed by Peter and Paul: lame people were healed, the dead were raised, and evil spirits were cast out.

Often when we think of miracles, we think only of some such wonder performed in the natural world. In America we wonder why we don't see more of these today. One answer may be that we (in the church) have been deeply influenced by the naturalistic teaching in our educational system. We try to explain everything in terms of natural phenomena. We only allow for God in such things as earthquakes, storms, and eruptions of volcanoes. These we call "acts of God." We fail to see God's miracles when we are spared serious injury in a terrible accident. We say, "My friend was 'lucky' " when overcome by deadly gas, but rescued by an observant farmhand, instead of saying, "God worked a miracle." The problem is that frequently we do not have eyes to see what God has done.

Godbey, Kinghorn, and Purkiser all believe that spiritual miracles are of even greater wonder than physical miracles. Godbey cites examples of Finney, Benjamin Abbott, one of Bishop Asbury's circuit riding preachers, as well as his own ministry, when God so came on the scene that many were converted. Finney walked into a cotton mill and never had a chance to say a word; people were knocked to the floor and began to call on God.

Many physical miracles we hear about today take place in mission lands, among people who are hearing the Gospel for the first time. But greater miracles are no doubt happening in the changed and transformed lives of people.

Those who refuse to believe unless a miracle or sign is performed are on the wrong foot. Jesus never accommodated Himself to these requests. He also warned the people of His day, "This generation is an evil generation; it seeks a sign" (Luke 11:29, RSV). Very few people became believers as a result of miracles in Jesus' day. Not many of the 5,000 truly followed Jesus. The raising of Lazarus didn't even convince them; in fact, the leaders went out and plotted to kill Jesus because of this miracle.

God can and does work miracles. He can work contrary to the laws of nature, but more frequently He works with the timing of His own natural laws. The car stalls for no apparent reason, but as we approach a crossroad, we see another car which should have stopped go speeding through. We recognize God has just performed a miracle. God's power is still at work in the changing of the spiritual nature of people. He raises those dead in trespasses and sins. He brings conviction to the heart of a hardened sinner by the smile of an innocent baby.

Christians should not spend a great amount of time fretting if physical miracles are not occurring in their lives or churches. We are called to walk by faith and not by sight. We believe God even when we do not see any outward demonstration of His working.

DIVINE HEALING

God does heal people in a miraculous way as the result of believing prayer. Many times in our chapel services at

Western Evangelical Seminary, we have received prayer requests for people who are ill. On several occasions we have seen God perform miracles. One young man called to the ministry had a brain tumor and was facing surgery. God healed him without surgery, and he was able to continue in his studies.

Godbey in his writings states, "Since the rise of the holiness movement, divine healing has become so common as to be no longer a matter of controversy." He cited several examples of people who were healed and were given additional years to serve God. He also cited a case when God did not give the gift of healing and took His servant home (W.B. Godbey, *Spiritual Gifts and Graces* [Cincinnati: M.W. Knapp, 1895], p. 25).

Purkiser points out that in 1 Corinthians 12:9, 28, 30, both gifts and healings are in the plural. His assessment is that there "is no generalized 'gift of healing' that can be exercised in favor of any and all who come. There are specific gifts for specific instances of healing" (W.T. Purkiser, *The Gifts of the Spirit* [Kansas City, Missouri: Beacon Hill Press, 1975], p. 42). Our observation agrees with this, both from the study of the biblical text and from what we have seen God do in the lives of people.

Great distress has come to God's people because some well-meaning, but misguided, people have taught that it is God's will to always heal. Some dear brothers and sisters in the faith have gone through dark days spiritually because they came to the conclusion that somehow they were lacking in faith or had some hidden sin which kept back God's healing. The well-meaning teachers have affirmed that divine healing is in the redemptive will of God. It is in this will that we find conversion and sanctification. We do believe that God has obligated Himself to hear and answer the prayer of any sinner who calls on Him for mercy. He has also obligated Himself to sanctify every believer who comes for cleansing and empowering.

We hold that divine healing is in the sovereign will of God rather than His redemptive will. (We recognize that sovereign will and redemptive will are theological terms, but they are helpful.) Since divine healing is in His sovereign will, He heals, He delays, or He refuses physical healing as He sees what is best for His servant. God may answer in one of several possible ways: (1) He may heal instantly. (2) He may heal through the natural processes He has built into the body. (3) He may heal through doctors and medicines. God gave these people these talents and the ability to discover cures. (4) He may say, "My grace is sufficient for you," as He did with His servant Paul (2 Cor. 12:7-10). In this instance, He gives grace to bear the affliction in a way that brings honor to God (John 9:3). (5) He may use the disease as a means to take His child home to be with Him. This is ultimate healing. Death has been conquered and is now servant to Jesus. It still rules over us but only at His permission.

Scripture teaches that we are to believe in Christ's *ability* to heal, not His *willingness* to heal (Mark 1:40ff; 9:15-29). So while we do not know God's will for this specific case, we can affirm that God has power to heal and that we want Him to work out His perfect will in the one who is ill. Godbey suggests that the person who is resigned and committed to the will of God will want God to choose what is best whether to live, suffer, or die. "When you make this perfect consecration, it is highly probable that God will see that He can use you for His glory in this world, and consequently prolong your life" (W.B. Godbey, *Spiritual Gifts and Graces* [Cincinnati: M.W. Knapp, 1895], pp. 30–31).

In commenting on James 5:14, Kinghorn points out, "The word James uses for 'anoint' is *aleipho*, which means 'to oil the skin by rubbing,' a medical practice common in the East. James does not use the word *chrio*, which means 'a ritualistic or symbolic anointing.' " Before the days of miracle drugs such as penicillin, rubbing with oil was one of the most widely accepted medical remedies known to man. I believe that the rubbing with oil to which James referred was a commonly accepted medical practice used on sick persons.

James was saying, in effect, "Use prayer and use the best medical know-how available—both methods of healing come from God. But do all 'in the name of the Lord,' for God is the source of all healing" (Kenneth C. Kinghorn, *Gifts of the Spirit* [Nashville: Abingdon, 1976], pp. 70–71). A sign erected by Tenwek Hospital in Kenya, East Africa says it well, "We treat; Jesus heals."

God does heal. At times He does the miraculous. In many of our churches in the Wesleyan tradition we need to make greater use of the gifts of healings.

EXORCISM

Exorcism is not in any of the New Testament gift lists. As we mentioned earlier, Paul used this ability on his missionary journeys. Exorcism could in many ways be considered as Part B of discernment of spirits. The two gifts usually go together. A correct understanding will help avoid some erroneous teachings.

First, we want to recognize the existence of demons and demon possession. Examples abound in Scripture. I have found many of the same types of things in Burundi in my missionary labors there. Second, we do not want to give them more credit than they deserve. A Christian can fall into sin and in no way be possessed by a demon. A Christian can suffer from mental illness and not be possessed. A Christian can be depressed and not possessed. These people need counsel and help, but not exorcism.

Another teaching we strongly disagree with is the suggestion that a Christian can be possessed by a demon. In the strongest terms possible we suggest that this can't be. In our search of Scripture we have not found one example to confirm this. It also disagrees with such statements as, "Does a fountain send out from the same opening both fresh and bitter water?" (James 3:11, NASB) "And if Satan casts out Satan, he is divided against himself. How then shall his kingdom stand? . . . But if I cast out demons by the Spirit of God, then the kingdom of God has come upon you" (Matt. 12:26, 28, NASB). It also is a logical impossibility. A demon spirit and the Holy Spirit cannot indwell the same personality. If one comes, the other will go. The greatest protection a Christian can have against demon possession is to be filled with the Holy Spirit. The Burundi found the Holy Spirit was totally adequate.

From my observation and study, the most frequent sources for demon possession are: (1) a deep involvement in occult practices, (2) heavy involvement in drugs, (3) involvement in Eastern religions where the mind is opened up to whatever might come, and (4) being born into a family that is involved in these things. However, just because someone has played around with these does not mean the person has become possessed. The possibilities are just greater where these characteristics are found. At seminars some women have suggested that sexual abuse may be another route for demon possession. I am searching for further evidence in this area.

Demon possession is a reality. It isn't as common a phenomenon as some overzealous souls believe, but is more common than some who relegate demons to superstitions of the past believe.

When there is reasonable proof that possession has taken place, believers should follow the teaching of Scripture and exorcise them in the powerful name of Jesus. Demons cannot stand before the blood of Jesus, God's Word, and the name of Jesus. Never attempt to do this by yourself. You should always gather together a group of Holy-Spirit-filled believers. Be prepared for a struggle and real wrestling in prayer. God is able: deliverance will come. In Burundi the church grew because people were delivered.

LANGUAGES AND INTERPRETATION

We come to the last two gifts we found in Scripture. These two gifts have caused much misunderstanding and strife in the church. Churches have gone through splits because of them. They have, at other times, been made the evidence of being filled with the Holy Spirit. It is because of these two gifts that many within evangelical churches have been fearful of any teaching on gifts. We don't want to either fear the gifts or have an unhealthy fascination with certain gifts. Either position would be contrary to the clear teaching of Scripture.

These two gifts have been interpreted variously by Bible expositors. To think we can offer an explanation that will satisfy all would be presumptive on our part. Let us, though, share with you our understanding as we have arrived at it through the study of Scripture and the writings of others.

On the Day of Pentecost when the Holy Spirit came upon the 120, purifying their hearts by faith, He gave the disciples the ability to speak languages they had never learned. There are sixteen different regions of the world mentioned, and they were all hearing the Gospel in their mother tongues. The people doing the speaking were Galileans. This caused the people to marvel. In our day we would say that the speakers were only country bumpkins who were uncultured people. There is no natural way by which they could speak foreign languages flawlessly, allowing the people to understand clearly the Word of God, but this is what happened. It appears to us that God was so anxious to get His Word out that He gave this gift to His people for evangelistic purposes.

We believe that this explanation (evangelism) will fit the other times in Acts when it is recorded that those filled with the Holy Spirit spoke in other languages. The soldiers under Cornelius came from various parts of the Roman Empire. They needed to hear God's miraculous doings in the house of Cornelius so they too could respond. A similar situation took place in Ephesus.

In Corinth it is harder to know all that was taking place. Paul certainly was distressed with their practices. We are not attempting to be dogmatic, but let us suggest what we believe was happening. Corinth was a cosmopolitan city. It is estimated that at one point Corinth had 700,000 residents; 200,000 were free and 500,000 were slaves. In Paul's time the city wasn't this large, but the characteristics were similar. These people came from many different language groups. Greek was the common language for trade, discussion, giving instructions, etc. Many of the slaves understood enough Greek to get saved. As they were blessed in a service, they testified using their mother tongues. They were freer to express themselves in this way. This was causing confusion in the services, so Paul instructed them that unless someone was there who could interpret what was said, they should refrain from speaking in a language others didn't understand.

Those who work in cross-cultural evangelism find this true today. People may know a "trade" language very well, but when they speak about what God has done in their hearts, they prefer to speak in their mother tongue. Likewise in times of prayer people switch to their mother tongue when they are desperate before God.

Commentaries written before 1900 agree that the tongues in Acts and Corinth were languages spoken on this earth. We have not found any suggestion of an "unknown" tongue or "prayer" language among the commentators. Liberalism, however, began to question this interpretation. They suggested that the believers in Corinth had been influenced by the mystery religions and that the people were speaking in ecstatic utterances similar to that found in paganism. While paganism has ever sought to influence Christianity, there is no good reason to believe this is what was happening at Corinth.

God has, on occasion, given this gift to those seeking to witness to people of a different language. This has been recorded in missionary journals and articles. The people have heard the Word accurately and responded to it. I never did receive this gift, though I asked God for it. Rather, I had to learn Kirundi the hard way. I believe God took my stumbling, flawed use of the Kirundi language and spoke it to the hearts of the Burundi in a way that brought them to the Savior. The Spirit helped me in my study of the Kirundi language. He helped me preach in it. He helped the people understand.

Linguistic ability may be considered a natural talent; God does take this and turn it into a spiritual gift for the communication and interpretation of His Word.

Nowhere in Scripture has this gift or any gift made the evidence of entire sanctification or being filled with the Holy Spirit. The Holy Spirit witnesses to the believer's heart so the person knows that the Spirit has come in His fullness. He does not give one gift to all as the evidence of His indwelling. Except for some radical groups, Pentecostal church bodies have come to this same conclusion. Some of the mainline Pentecostal churches are again calling their people to the earlier position; they feel they have left their roots.

Sign gifts are sensational; they catch the attention of the people. God gives these gifts to some within the body. On some occasions they have caused people to turn to God. These gifts have brought glory to God, but unfortunately they have also brought division to His people. If gifts cause division, people are getting out of the will of God. Within the great variety of churches today, one should find a group that teaches Scripture in a way that you feel is true. If the group does not agree with your interpretation, you do not have freedom or authority to cause division by a big disagreement on a gift. Leave peacefully and find a group compatible to your personal findings.

 DISCUSSION
1. Do you believe sign gifts are operating today?
2. Have you ever witnessed a counterfeit use of sign gifts?
3. Based on chapter 7 write a paragraph that expresses your views about sign gifts.

 APPLICATION
Plan to have a discussion with your pastor and get his/her insights on the subject of sign gifts.

CHAPTER 8

Steps in Finding Your Gift(s)

The Bible gives us lists of the gifts. We see how some of the people used their gifts, but it does not give us a detailed account as to how to determine our gift(s). Most books on spiritual gifts have a chapter on "Discovering Your Spiritual Gift." Kinghorn suggests six steps, Wagner and Yohn have five steps, and Flynn has seven. We are not making any claim to originality in this book; if there is any uniqueness it is in the way we have put them together. We will make use of material produced by Kinghorn, but will feel free to draw on others when they are helpful.

PREREQUISITES FOR DISCOVERY

Certain prerequisites must be present before you begin your discovery of spiritual gifts. First of all, you must be a child of God. God gives natural talents to all people in this world, but He only gives spiritual gifts to His children. A person can become a member of a church and not be a child of God. One enters the family of God through the new birth experience (John 3:1-16). If this has not yet taken place in your life, then you need to seek God until you have been born into His family by faith.

God gives gifts to those who are born again, but immature in the faith. This is obvious from the things that happened at Corinth. In our Wesleyan tradition, we encourage people to go on and be sanctified by the infilling of the heart with the Holy Spirit. We suggest that if you have not yet experienced this deepened relationship in the Lord that you seek God until it is yours. Gifts can be used in a carnal way that cause division and strife. Gifts were not given with this purpose in mind. They were given rather to be used to build up the body of Christ. Spirit-filled believers who are using their gifts can do the greater good for God.

Second, you need to believe that spiritual gifts are for today. If you believe that gifts were only for the apostles or early church, then there is little point in your continued search. If you, however, believe as we do that God still gives gifts to people today, then continue on. If you aren't sure, we would encourage you to go back and study the various biblical passages in chapter 2 until you are convinced. You need to believe that God gives at least one gift to every member of the family of God.

Third, you must be willing to put out effort in the discovery of your gift(s). The steps we will outline constitute a spiritual exercise. If spiritually you want to sit in the shade of a tree sipping iced tea, you will not discover your gift. You must be willing to roll up your sleeves and go to work.

Fourth, you need to pray. James tells us in 1:5, "If any of you lacks wisdom, he should ask God, who gives generously to all without finding fault, and it will be given to him." Ask God to make it clear to you. Be willing to listen to God. Wait and do not become discouraged if you haven't found it in the first twenty-four hour period.

Spiritual gifts, like natural talents, are usually discovered as one matures in Christian discipleship. It will take time to identify and begin to use the spiritual gifts God has given. Young people from believing families, as well as young Christians, should not despair if they haven't found their spiritual gift within six months of their conversion. Remember God is more interested in what you are than what you do for Him. He is at work bringing you into conformity with His own holy character. Submit to this process of refinement. God is working to bring you to the place where you can be most effective for Him.

CULTIVATE AN OPENNESS TO THE HOLY SPIRIT

In discovering spiritual gifts, be open to God for what He wants to do through you. Remember that the Holy Spirit resides in you. It is He who gives the gift(s). If the Holy Spirit is not present, there will be no spiritual gifts. Cultivate an openness, a receptivity, and an obedience to Him. The only attitude that is proper is a willing surrender to His gracious working. Daily submission to Him for His use will produce the conditions necessary for the discovery and use of spiritual gifts.

As you open yourself up to the Holy Spirit, pray, and study the gifts in Scripture, you should learn your church's position on gifts. There is not universal agreement on teaching regarding spiritual gifts. We believe strongly in the body of Christ and are committed to it. When you voluntarily join a church, you submit yourself to its discipline and authority. The pastor is the head shepherd and in a special way is held responsible for the congregation. You should be loyal to this church with its beliefs and practices and submit to the one who has been

named pastor. If you cannot do this, then leave respect-
fully and ask God to lead you to another fellowship
which is in greater harmony with your beliefs and practice. Wagner is correct when he writes,

> Notice, the thing I do not recommend is that you
> decide to stay where you are and try to convince the
> church or certain individuals in it that they should
> change their position. . . . God did not give spiritual
> gifts for dissension and hard feelings. He gave spiri-
> tual gifts to enhance the health and vitality and
> growth of the Body. Every unit of spiritual energy
> being used to fight battles over spiritual gifts is one
> unit that cannot be used for reaching out to lost men
> and women. I believe that God prefers our energies
> to be used in seeing that the lost are found and that
> the church grows (C. Peter Wagner, *Your Spiritual
> Gifts Can Help Your Church Grow* [Glendale, Califor-
> nia: Regal, 1974], p. 118).

The Word of God does not give you permission to use
gifts to cause division and strife.

EXAMINE YOUR DESIRES IN CHRISTIAN SERVICE

Kinghorn suggests examining your aspirations for Christian service and ministry. Look at the things you feel
drawn to. It would be well to review the list of gifts and
the explanations offered. What on that list sparks your
interest? What sounds interesting to you?

There is a notion abroad that God's will and His service
is something like a bitter pill. We have to do it but we
don't like it. This certainly is a teaching of the enemy to
keep people from gladly serving the Lord. When our will
is submitted to God's will, it is a delight to do His will and

to serve Him. Doing the will of God brings happiness and contentment. God's normal way of working in our lives is to bring excitement and challenge, not boredom.

God creates within us desires. These become His leadings to give us direction (Phil. 2:13; Ps. 37:4). His ways are the ways of fulfillment and joy. We do well to pay attention to those inner aspirations and desires. These frequently are the leading of the Holy Spirit. God gets so much better service from those who gladly serve Him with hearts full of excitement than He does from those who do something from a sense of duty only. There is nothing spiritually wrong with the person who is happy and serving the Lord.

IDENTIFY NEEDS IN THE CHURCH

Identify the needs within the body, says Kinghorn. Wagner suggests experimenting with as many of the gifts as you can. Kinghorn's suggestion is based more on subjective feelings of need as you see them in the church. Wagner's suggestion is to try out some of the items you feel drawn to. Not all of the gifts can be experimented with, but some of the very essential ones are available for such experimentation: evangelism, teaching, pastoring, service, mercy, hospitality, music, and craftsmanship.

If you examine the needs of the church and find you are concerned about the level of instruction or knowledge, God may be giving you the gift of teaching. If you are concerned about the needs of those who are emotionally or physically hurting, you may have the gift of mercy. If you see that certain gifted people are limited because of detail work they need to take care of, you may have the gift of helps. If you are concerned for the people of God because they are misled, confused, or divided, you may have the gift of pastor. If you are concerned about disorganization and mismanagement, you may have the gift of administration. If you are concerned because God's work is limited as a result of lack of funds, you may have the gift of giving. We could go on.

Check your concerns. God is probably helping you discover your spiritual gifts through the needs you see. As you become involved, you will find that God has gifted you with the necessary gifts in order to carry out the ministry.

EVALUATE YOUR EXPERIENCES IN SERVICE

Evaluate your feelings as well as the results of your effort to serve and minister. The first time you do something, your heart may be pounding so hard you think everyone can hear it. How did you feel afterward? Even though you were scared, did you enjoy it or did you dread it? There is no conflict between serving the Lord and finding satisfaction in it.

If what you are doing is a gift from God, your effectiveness will increase with usage. Kinghorn suggests three questions to ask yourself: (1) Am I developing more competence in this area? (2) Do opportunities open up for me to exercise this gift? (3) Are my efforts producing good results in the lives of others? (Kenneth C. Kinghorn, *Gifts of the Spirit* [Nashville: Abingdon, 1976], p. 112). A proper usage of spiritual gifts will result in an increase in confidence, ability, and effectiveness. A good sign that God has gifted you with a particular gift is that others within the church will be helped by your ministry.

CONFIRMATION FROM OTHER BELIEVERS

Expect confirmation from the body of Christ. Often others will notice your spiritual gift before you become aware of it. If no one else within the body senses that you have been gifted in a particular area, then you may need to keep looking.

Gifts are to be exercised within the body. It is necessary to be part of a fellowship. We cannot develop into strong mature Christians in isolation. We need each other. So while gifts are discovered in ministering to the body, the body plays an important role in affirming those gifts. We are not seeking to build our egos, but we can help a brother or sister in the Lord by sharing with them how we have been helped through the exercising of their gift. This will give them direction as well as encouragement.

Gifts are manifested primarily within the family of God. All the discussions on spiritual gifts occur in the New Testament in relationship to the body of Christ. As Christians we need each other. We need to work together in harmony. Christ is the Head; we are the various members that make up the body of Christ. No Christian will have all the gifts. We need the other members of the body of Christ to be complete. A few of the gifts will be used primarily among non-Christians. Apostleship, evangelism, and missionary fit this category. Even these gifts will be recognized by the body and affirmed.

If the Christian community consistently recognizes and receives your ministry, you may be sure God is working in you through your spiritual gift.

Several different tools have been developed to assist people in discovering their spiritual gifts. A tool that fits with teaching given in this book was prepared by Donald Hohensee of Western Evangelical Seminary. It is entitled, "Spiritual Gifts and Church Growth Wesley Questionnaire." A copy of this tool appeared between chapters 1 and 2. Additional copies are available from Charles E. Fuller Institute, P.O. Box 91990, Pasadena, California 91109-1990, (818) 449-0425. When ordering request the

"Wesley Spiritual Gifts Questionnaire," item C110.

If you have not yet filled out the questionnaire, it would be good for you to do so at the conclusion of this chapter. If you have followed the suggestions outlined in this lesson and haven't yet discovered your spiritual gift, do not become discouraged. Just keep walking with God and be obedient to Him. Remember He is more interested in what we are than what we do for Him. In His time He will make it clear to you, and you will find real joy and satisfaction.

RESULTS OF DISCOVERY AND USE

What happens if the members of the church discover, develop, and use their spiritual gifts? You will find a growing church that is working together in beautiful harmony. The people will feel free, and they will find delight and happiness in serving within the body.

A knowledge of your gift(s) will help you know your place within the body. You will know your job description. You should serve the Lord spending most of your time in those areas in which He has gifted you. As we indicated earlier, in an emergency we serve the Lord even in areas in which we are not gifted; we help out as we can.

When we serve the Lord according to our gifts, the members will work together in love and harmony. In my body there is no conflict between my right hand and my left hand, so in the body of Christ there should not be conflict. We recognize that we need each other, and we work for the advancement of the body. This will be spelled out in greater detail in the chapters that follow.

A proper understanding of gifts will knock down pride. They are gifts, given by God at His discretion. It will avoid false humility. God has given the gift and He expects us to use it as good stewards. It will reduce envy. If God gives them, then He gives to each one what He feels best and so there is no ground for jealousy, strife, or envy. It removes false guilt; if God has not gifted us in an area, we just recognize this and go on.

The whole body will mature as a result of proper usage. The church will grow in the Lord and others will be added to it. Last of all, God will be glorified.

What happens if I don't bother to discover my gift? Or I discover but fail to develop the gift God has given?

First Peter 4:10 teaches that I am a steward of the gift(s) God has given me. Matthew 25:14-30 teaches that if I use my gift well, I am a good steward. If I don't use my gift well, I am a wicked, lazy servant and in the end I will be cast out.

Charles Swindoll wrote,

The Springfield, Oregon, Public Schools Newsletter published an article that caught my eye some time ago. As I read it, it struck me that I was reading a parable of familiar frustration in the Christian home and Body of Christ today.

Once upon a time, the animals decided they should do something meaningful to meet the problems of the new world. So they organized a school.

They adopted an activity curriculum of running, climbing, swimming, and flying. To make it easier to administer the curriculum, all the animals took all the subjects.

The *duck* was excellent in swimming: in fact, better than his instructor. But he made only passing grades in flying, and was very poor in running. Since he was slow in running, he had to drop swimming and stay after school to practice running. This caused his webbed feet to be badly worn, so that he was only average in swimming. But average was quite acceptable, so nobody worried about that except the duck.

The *rabbit* started at the top of his class in running, but developed a nervous twitch in his leg muscles because of so much make-up work in swimming.

The *squirrel* was excellent in climbing, but he encountered constant frustration in flying class because his teacher made him start from the ground up instead of from the treetop down. He developed "charlie horses" from overexertion, and so only got a C in climbing and a D in running.

The *eagle* was a problem child and was severely disciplined for being a non-conformist. In climbing classes he beat all the others to the top of the tree, but insisted on using his own way to get there. . . . (Charles R. Swindoll, *Growing Strong in the Seasons of Life* [Portland, Oregon: Multnomah Press, 1983], p. 312).

This fable illustrates for us what we want to accomplish by this teaching on spiritual gifts. We want people to be free and to function in those areas where they have been gifted by God. In the church, it becomes counter-productive to chain people's energies in activities for which they are not gifted.

 DISCUSSION
1. Mark your spiritual gifts questionnaire.
2. Think through the prerequisites given in chapter 8.
3. How many of these prerequisites have you met?

 APPLICATION
With the results of your spiritual gifts questionnaire, review the five steps for discovering your spiritual gifts.

Keep your highest gifts in mind as you read chapter 9.

Your Spiritual Gifts in Relation to the Church

I t is our goal in this chapter to discover the relationships between spiritual gifts and the local church. To do this, we need to have a general understanding of what the ministry of the church is, or what the church's philosophy of ministry is.

Before we move to a formal study of a philosophy of ministry, we need to call your attention to one of the unique points of this book, *Your Spiritual Gifts and Your Local Church.* Our emphasis is "your"—your gift, your church.

Dr. Hohensee and I would again invite you to turn to the Wesley Spiritual Gifts Questionnaire which has been placed between chapters 1 and 2. This is a good time to mark the questions, review chapter 8, and identify your gifts to discover your ministry in your church.

The dictionary states this definition for philosophy: "A critical study of fundamental beliefs and the grounds for them; the sum of ideas and convictions of an individual or group." Using this definition as a guide, what do we fundamentally believe the church "is"? What do we basically believe the church is to be "doing"? And how can these beliefs, ideas, and convictions become a reality?

I believe this philosophy can take shape as we answer these questions: What is the role of the church? What is the goal of the church? What is the cost to reach the goal and fulfill the role of the church? How can we begin to take the idea of the church and make it tangible and practical for everyday use?

Before moving into a study of the gift passages in order to build a statement of purpose, I would like to state a more general definition of the church. A literal definition would be the church is an assembly of called out ones. This simple statement places the emphasis on people, not buildings.

At one of our coffee cup consultations, Dr. Hohensee and I addressed this concept. The church where I was ministering was experiencing rapid growth. We had the "best" church in the Portland metro area, and I wanted as many people as possible to be touched by our services. "Let's double the program." "Let's build a new sanctuary." I wanted the pastor to get with it and lead us into a building program. After I enthusiastically expressed my great philosophy, Don reminded me that it is people first; program second; buildings third. He was right. The church is "called out people."

For the purpose of our study, let's review the main Scriptures we have studied on spiritual gifts. Romans 12:4-5: "Just as each of us has one body with many members, and these members do not all have the same function, so in Christ we who are many form one body, and each member belongs to all the others."

Look at 1 Corinthians 12:12: "The body is a unit, though it is made up of many parts; and though all its parts are many, they form one body. So it is with Christ."

The last major section of Scripture is Ephesians 4:16: "From Him the whole body, joined and held together by every supporting ligament, grows and builds itself up in love as each part does its work."

I am sure you can see the same concept developing that I did: the concept of the body. Now turn to Ephesians 5:23; this phrase leaps up, "Christ is the Head of the church, His body, of which He is the Savior." The narration of this passage is beautiful and informative. The church is the body; the church is the object of His love. This passage picks up the metaphor or word picture of the husband's love for his wife, just as Christ loved the church. He (Christ) gave Himself for her, to make her holy, radiant, and blameless. Even though it is not stated as such, the church is the bride of Christ. Verse 32 states, "This is a profound mystery—but I am talking about Christ and the church."

The church is the body of Christ, and the bride. This truth is the beginning of our philosophy. This is the first step in making something that is intangible, tangible. All of the Gospel accounts of the earthly ministry of Jesus come to bear here: He came to seek and to save, not to be ministered unto, but to minister.

Cathedral films in their Life of Christ series gives this account that illustrates for us the importance of this concept. It is the account of Jesus touching the leper. In the distance you can hear the sound of small bells ringing. At first you don't pay much attention, until you hear someone say "Lepers" and the crowd quickly moves off the road to let them pass. The leper steps forward and kneels in front of Jesus. As the disciples express horror and fear, Jesus reaches out and touches the leper. What a practical example. Just as the hand of Jesus ministered to the leper, we as a church become His hands, His body for ministry.

Now we know that we are the body. Do you feel or

emotionally believe you're part of the body of Christ? Do you feel you are the bride, the object of His love? The challenge of this truth is "Let's act like we're part of the body of Christ," in attitude and ministry.

What is the goal of the church? What is the purpose of the church? What is the church supposed to be doing? In general terms, we are to glorify God in all we say and do. Paul in 2 Corinthians 3 states that we are to reflect His glory—also 1 Corinthians 10:31, "Do it all for the glory of God." But more specifically, in Ephesians 4:13 the purpose of the church and the purpose of the operation of the gifts is to bring people to the place of maturity. Use this same passage, "attaining to the whole measure of the fullness of Christ," or until we become like Jesus.

From the Wesleyan viewpoint, this means that a person is born again (John 3:16) and is born of the Spirit. As we grow in grace, there comes a time when Romans 12:1-2 becomes an act of faith on our part. We surrender our lives to Christ. We ask the Spirit to cleanse us and possess us, and we recognize the lordship of Christ. This recognition of Christ as Lord leads us toward a deeper understanding of Christian maturity and affects one's attitudes and motives. Paul again says in Ephesians 4:15, "We will in all things grow up into Him who is the Head, that is, Christ." I really believe verses 23 and 24 of the chapter summarize this concept:

To be made new in the attitude of your minds; and to put on the new self, created to be like God in true righteousness and holiness.

The purpose of the church is to bring people to maturity in Christ. Christian maturity is a growing relationship with the Lord and a developing relationship with other individuals. Christian maturity does not stop with entire sanctification. Entire sanctification intensifies our desire to be like Jesus and to live a life of holiness.

To bring this purpose into focus, we now state three goals: Bring people to Christ (Acts 2:40); build people up in Christ (1 Cor. 14:26); and prepare people to serve in Christ (Eph. 4:12). The Great Commission as stated in Matthew 28:18-20 would be the simplest way to state these goals: making disciples; baptizing; teaching.

I am sure that you have noticed that all through our study we have stayed in the scriptural context of the spiritual gifts. This draws us to the conclusion that our understanding of spiritual gifts becomes part of our philosophy of ministry. In the growth process, the church should enable you to discover your spiritual gifts and offer you training and a place to serve.

In our desire to develop a philosophy of ministry, we have established a general purpose. This general purpose is to enable the Christian to grow to maturity in Christ. The goals that are factors in realizing this purpose are bringing people to Christ, building people up in Christ, and enabling people to serve in Christ. I feel there is still another level of study in defining the general purpose of the church, and that is the elements. The dictionary definition of element is "a component, part, or quantity, often one that is basic or essential."

I believe there are seven elements that can be isolated from Scripture that are essential for a proper balance in reaching our goals in order to fulfill our purpose. For the purpose of our study, I would like to list these seven elements, cite a Scripture, and give a short definition:

Evangelism—Acts 2:40
Calling people to repentance and to be reconciled to God.
Teaching—Acts 2:42

Systematic presentation of truth.

Fellowship — Acts 2:42

Partnership or participation.

Worship — Acts 2:42

Worship is adoration, reverence, which in this context is the Lord's Supper.

Prayer — Acts 2:42

Prayer is communion with God.

Learning — 1 Corinthians 14:31

Relationship, modeling of truth; task-oriented.

Service — Ephesians 4:12

Servant ministry.

These seven elements will appear at different times, places, and through different agencies. The important idea is that they are needed to bring balance in reaching our goals in order to fulfill our purpose.

To help clarify this idea of the purpose of the church in relationship to goals and elements, a biblical systems model has been designed to illustrate this concept. What I believe we have in the systems model is a visual method of developing a statement of purpose which follows a proper management by objective strategy. The model is given as Illustration 1. Along with the model, an evaluation/planning form has been included as Illustration 2. I have found this systems model and evaluation/planning form very useful in planning a workable local church program.

Before sharing a simple formula on how the model works, I would like to state a definition of systems given by Drs. Lindgren and Shawchuck in their book *Management for Your Church:* "An organizational system is a set of components that work together to accomplish an overall objective (purpose)."

As you look at the model the flow would move through a series of questions like these:

I. PURPOSE — How does this contribute to our purpose?

II. GOALS — How does this activity help us reach our three stated general goals?

III. ELEMENTS — Which of the elements (one or two) are being intregrated by this activity?

IV. AGENCIES — Which of the present agencies can best carry out this activity, or is a new agency necessary?

V. SETTING — What is the best setting to use for the selected agency to integrate the selected element to reach a general goal which ultimately moves the individual toward the stated purpose?

All this is necessary to develop a philosophy of ministry: purpose, goals, and elements. A philosophy should be a statement that answers these questions:

1. What is the reason for our church's existence?
2. What are the characteristics of our church's lifestyle?
3. What does our church expect of its members?
4. What will our church's plan of ministry be?
5. What will be the specific style of our services?

Now let's answer that third question as we continue our development in understanding the spiritual gifts and the local church. What is the cost? What will it take to reach the goals to fulfill the purpose?

One of the most obvious costs, and many times the one that is not faced, is _____? What do you think it is? It is one of the secrets of success. No, it is not money. It is WORK! Yes, strenuous activity that involves difficulty and effort. Now the operation of spiritual gifts will make the work meaningful, yet there will be an investment of time and energy.

A BIBLICAL SYSTEMS APPROACH TO MINISTRY

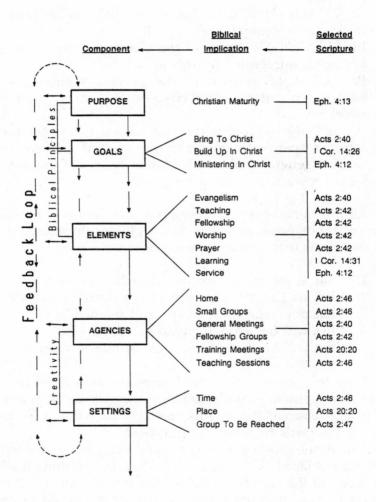

Illustration 1

EVALUATION AND PLANNING FORM FOR MINISTRY

Primary Emphasis
ELEMENTS
Rate A, B, C

Various agencies and settings of the church which relate to adults.	EVANGELISM	TEACHING	WORSHIP	FELLOWSHIP	SERVICE	PRAYER	LEARNING
Sunday School							
Sunday Morning Service							
Sunday Evening Service							
Midweek Prayer/Bible Study							
Revival Services							
Retreats							
Small Group Bible Studies							
Social Events							
Evangelical Men							
Evangelical Women							
Leadership Development							
Discipling							

EVALUATION

Check appropriate box as to how this sheet is being used.

PLANNING

Illustration 2

133

Another cost that needs to be addressed that is alluded to in Ephesians 5:21 is submission—submission to others in the body. This cost factor allows for the body to function and each individual part to contribute to the welfare of the whole.

Let's move to the third cost, the cost of commitment. We quite often say we need commitment. This is true, but what do we mean by commitment? Ray Ortlund, while he was pastor at Lake Avenue Congregational Church in Pasadena, set forth three levels of commitment: first, toward God; second, toward the family of God; and third, toward God's work. There is a commitment that Christ is Lord; second, commitment to the body of Christ; and third, commitment to the work of Christ, that in all of life we recognize the lordship of Christ by giving Him preeminence and practicing His presence, that we guard the unity of the Spirit in our local body, that our lifestyle be one of godly influence and good works. In this consideration of commitment, we need to emphasize the order of priorities. Priority one is commitment to Christ; priority two is commitment to the body; and priority three is commitment to service.

I have experienced two examples of this principle of commitment—one negative and one positive.

There was a couple in a church where I pastored. For our illustration we will call them Jan and Herb. We were a small growing church so when Jan and Herb showed up one Sunday morning at church they were noticed and appreciated. The next week I called and discovered a couple that loved God and wanted to serve the Lord. Well, true to form, Jan and Herb became very active in our church. Herb was a trustee and drove a Sunday School bus. Jan was active in women's ministry and taught a Sunday School class.

After about two years Jan and Herb left our church. I

called on them and tried to see what caused them to withdraw. I found they loved the Lord and wanted to serve Him, so I knew spiritually there was no problem. But later in the conversation I discovered they were not committed to the body of believers with whom they were worshiping and serving. Jan and Herb didn't come to small group activities or tarry after church and visit with other members of the fellowship. They were not committed to the body. Therefore there was nothing to hold them to that fellowship.

A few years later I was visiting with a layperson who was deeply involved in the church where I was serving. I asked him what he thought was the secret to our church's growth. He shared several exciting things that the church was doing. This church prayed together, worked together, and fellowshipped together. He shared how a group of workers made a commitment to God and to each other to build a great church for the glory of God, and it was happening.

As this study on our philosophy of ministry has developed, a natural introduction to a philosophy of spiritual gifts has taken place. It is exciting to see how the major Scripture passages on gifts identify the role and goals of the local church. In a very real sense, the local church reaches its full potential as the Holy Spirit is allowed to administer His gifts. It may be stated this way: Understanding spiritual gifts then is the key to understanding the purpose of the church.

I believe the best way to conclude this chapter is to cite a model statement of purpose. The model may help your fellowship as it begins to develop its own statement of purpose. Please keep in mind that it takes time to develop a statement of purpose. It needs to spring from a Bible study. It needs to reflect your fellowship's doctrinal distinctives.

STATEMENT OF PURPOSE

To glorify God by being mature disciples of Christ: by attracting and leading the unsaved to eternal hope through faith in the Lord Jesus Christ, encouraging Christians to consecrate themselves to God, and providing a climate for spiritual growth which equips gifted, Spirit-filled believers for worship and a dynamic ministry, using their gifts in serving our Jerusalem, Judea, and the world.

 DISCUSSION

1. Using Illustration 2 take an inventory of how well your church is covering the seven elements listed in the illustration.

2. Now using Illustration 2, how would you reorganize your local church program to incorporate these seven elements?

 APPLICATION

If you don't have a statement of purpose for your church, make an appointment with your pastor and see if he/she could use a key person to help write a statement.

CHAPTER 10

The Role
of the Local Church to
Your Ministry

—My church determines what ministries are needed. Agree; Disagree.
—My church calls individuals to participate in ministry. Agree; Disagree.
—My authority in ministry comes from the church. Agree; Disagree.

I f you agree with these three statements, you are an exceptional individual. The idea that the church determines, the church calls, and the church gives authority for many of us is different. In fact, I have found in many cases it is difficult to think this way.

I remember the first time I shared this concept with a group of young adults. We had broken into small groups to discuss the Scripture involved with the concept, and I was making a summary statement. One of the class members looked at me, saying, "You've got to be kidding."

First of all, I admitted this concept was causing me to stretch. As a group we found out that our concept of the church was too small, and rightfully so; we felt our official board was not as spiritually mature as they could be. Therefore, we were reluctant to place ourselves under their authority. Because of this, I am calling attention to the church's responsibility in ministry as well as our own personal responsibility.

I personally believe there are two steps in working our way through this study on what is the role of the church in our spiritual ministry. The first one we have considered in a previous study on our philosophy of the church. The second step is to examine significant Bible passages that deal with the role of the church in an individual's ministry. This second step will be the focus of this chapter.

First, let's review some conclusions from our study on the philosophy of the church. Remember, the church's role is that it is the body of Christ. The goal of the church is to win people to Christ, to build people up in Christ, and to give opportunity to serve in Christ. The cost factor is commitment: commitment to Christ, to the body, and then to service. All of these conclusions are drawn from Scripture. This chapter's focus is to see this philosophy applied to "my" spiritual gifts and "my" ministry. Many studies on spiritual gifts have been conducted in a parachurch setting, but our study is in a local church setting. I am aware of the idea that a parachurch organization works alongside of the local church, but the local church should be our focus.

In a local church setting we know the members—they're our friends; they're even human. Because of this we find it difficult to follow the principles that will be shared in this chapter. But I really believe that the local church setting is the real biblical model. To separate the study of spiritual gifts from the local church is to create a non-biblical concept of ministry. Jesus Christ is divine/human, Scripture is divine/human, and the church is divine/human;

therefore, a study of spiritual gifts and the local church is consistent with Christian doctrine.

In taking this second step, let's remember that Scripture is our "rule for faith and conduct." Scripture is our corrective to prevent us from going off to the right or left. In review, our Bible study focus has led to these conclusions:

— Every member is gifted.

— Every member is a steward of these gifts.

— We will be held accountable for the use of these gifts.

— The gifts are given to individuals for the proper functioning of the body.

Let's move ahead now and explore some key passages in Acts and Ephesians and see what key principles govern the use of an individual's spiritual gifts in the local church. The plan for developing this Bible study will be to list the passage, describe the situation in the passage, then isolate the principles that are applicable to the life of the church today.

Acts 1:14-26; 6:1-5. In Acts 1:14-26 we have the account of the early church selecting someone to take the place of Judas. The spiritual climate for this meeting was ideal: the group was of one mind and devoted to prayer. Then Peter, motivated by a desire to fulfill Scripture, led the fellowship in selecting a replacement for Judas. The dynamics of this special election are refreshing. There is the dynamic of following the Scripture. Note the dynamic of following the scriptural qualifications for this new candidate in verses 21 and 22. Note, how dynamic the spirit of prayer is in verses 24 and 25. This passage caused me to reevaluate the role of elections in a local church fellowship. When an election is conducted with the same concern to fulfill Scripture and is saturated in prayer, God can take a "human" vote and fulfill His divine will.

The account in Acts 6:1-5 is a good illustration of a church operating by "management by objective" princi-

139

ples. A felt need arose because of growth (v. 1). Their response was in light of their objective to "devote themselves to prayer and the ministry of the Word." Verse 3 states the qualification and verse 5 states the method of selection.

The principles that may be lifted from these passages are:

—Needs were determined by Scripture and by the objectives of the fellowship.

—The church fellowship established some basic requirements.

—The church selected or called individuals to participate in ministry.

—There was a oneness of mind or purpose.

—There was a spirit of prayer.

—There was the dynamic of praying and voting (divine/human).

Let's move to another passage—Acts 9:23-29; 13:1-2. The situation in Acts 9 describes the difficulty Paul had in getting established in the church. Here was a man who had gifts, but because of his previous lifestyle, the church did not receive him with open arms. Verses 27 and 28 become very strategic in our exploration for principles that govern the relationship of spiritual gifts and the local church. This is the way the verses read: "But Barnabas took hold of him and brought him to the apostles. He told them how Saul on his journey had seen the Lord and that the Lord had spoken to him, and how in Damascus he had preached fearlessly in the name of Jesus. So Saul stayed with them and moved about freely in Jerusalem, speaking boldly in the name of the Lord."

The next reference in this grouping is Acts 13:1-2. What a change. The church through its leadership set Barnabas and Paul aside for a special ministry. I must admit I thought a gifted man like Paul would have told the church where he was going to serve. What commitment on the part of Paul to let this group of humans tell him where to serve! Who am I to say I am above the leadership of my local church.

The principles that may be lifted from these references in Acts 9 and 13 are:

—The church confirms the spiritual gifts of the individual.

—There is a need for a time of supervision and probation.

THE CHURCH DETERMINES THE AREAS OF MINISTRY

Acts 15. This passage seems to be giving us a very human picture of the early church. Note the expressions of "sharp dispute and debate" in verse 2. Did you notice in verse 24 that some self-appointed people were ministering without the authority of the church? This account is very honest in that it shares the personal disagreements in that early church. But the motive of Christian love and concern surfaces in verses 19 and 28. Verse 28 sums up this concern: "It seemed good to the Holy Spirit and to us not to burden you with anything beyond the following requirements." One of the results of this account is that the group was "encouraged and strengthened" (see v. 32), which is the primary purpose in the ministry of spiritual gifts.

The principles that may be cited from this account are:

—The church commissions people to specific tasks.

—Specific ministry may be refused certain individuals who are gifted but thought not to be qualified.

There are two references that would be appropriate for use to those concerned now. Acts 6:6: "They presented these men to the apostles, who prayed and laid their hands on them." Acts 13:3: "So after they had fasted and prayed, they placed their hands on them and sent them off." These acts of commission were done in public. These simple acts seemed to communicate to the congregation and the candidate authority and responsibility. The principles that are lifted from these two verses could be:

—The authority in service is a given authority.

—Authority is given to the person who holds that position of service.

Ephesians 4:11-16. We have looked at this passage before, but it is very strategic in discovering the role of the church in relation to spiritual gifts.

The context of Ephesians 4 is spiritual gifts. The death and resurrection of Christ gave Him power and authority to give "gifts to men" (v. 8). I believe verse 12 sums up, at least for this study, the relationship of the church and our spiritual gifts. "To prepare God's people for works of service, so that the body of Christ may be built up." "Equipping for service" became a very key phrase in this study. In analyzing the word "equip" we see that this is "preparing for a specific task." It is very legitimate to conclude that the body has equipping gifts to prepare with specific serving gifts. But let's list the principle that gives light to our study:

—The receiving of gifts is a result of our salvation.

—The church is to equip people for a specific ministry.

As we conclude this study on the role of the church and spiritual gifts, let's just list the principles we have discovered:

—Needs were determined by Scripture and by the objectives of the fellowship.

—The church fellowship established some basic requirements.

—The church selected or called individuals to participate in ministry.

—There was a oneness of mind and purpose.

—There was a spirit of prayer.

—There was the dynamic of praying and voting (divine/human).

—The church confirms the gifts of the individual.

—There is a need for a time of supervision and probation.

—The church commissions people to a specific task.

—Specific ministry may be refused certain individuals.

—The authority in service is a given authority.

—Authority is given to the person who holds that position of service.

—The receiving of gifts is a result of our salvation.

—The church is to equip people for a specific ministry.

These principles all grow out of the definition of spiritual gifts established in chapter 2, "A Good Foundation."

A spiritual gift is a unique capacity given by the Holy Spirit to each believer for service/ministry within and to the body of Christ so that it can grow in quality, quantity, and organically.

Your spiritual gift is not given in a vacuum, but is given within the context of a local church.

I believe Ephesians 4:16 pulls all of these principles together. It also states a proper conclusion for this study:

"From Him the whole body, joined and held together by every supporting ligament, grows and builds itself up in love, as each part does its work."

This reference in Ephesians 4:16 seems to be the corrective to our study on gifts.

Many times a pastor will share with me that he is gifted in prophecy and will neglect the serving aspect of his church. Or a pastor gifted in service will neglect the prophetic area of his ministry. This passage simply says that many times we need to do *whatever* is needed to build each other up in love. The overriding emphasis is to serve in unity and love.

DISCUSSION

1. Design a chart that lists the six Bible passages given in chapter 10. Then match the eight principles given in chapter 10 with the six verses.

2. Discuss with another member of your church how your church would change if Ephesians 4:16 was the primary focus of spiritual gifts.

3. How do you think your church could help you use your spiritual gifts more effectively?

 APPLICATION

How would this statement change your ministry?

"Your spiritual gift is not given in a vacuum, but is given within the context of a local church."

CHAPTER 11

Organization
and Structure

T he general purposes of this chapter are to express reasons for organizing the church for ministry, using spiritually gifted people, and then to suggest a working organizational model which is based on spiritually gifted people.

It seems appropriate at this time to state a suggested definition of organization. A definition would read like this:

ORGANIZATION is the vehicle which carries the program toward its PURPOSE. It provides the machinery for cooperative effort on the part of people. It is not the purpose in itself, but is the means of achieving the purpose.

A good example of practical management by purpose or objective in a local church happened to me while working with Pastor Jim Marshall at the Oregon City Evangelical Church. Pastor Marshall and I were in the hall greeting people after church. A lady came directly up to me with a very intent look and said, "Allen, you know what our church needs?" I responded, glancing at the pastor, "No, what?" Very seriously she responded, "A bowling team."

I really didn't know how to respond. I felt like saying, "Yes, like we need a hole in the head!"

When I shared her concern with the pastor, he very wisely said, "How does that fit in with our statement of purpose?" That was all I needed to give a proper response to a very serious suggestion.

I reviewed the statement of purpose, which is similar to the one in chapter 9. We felt a bowling team was not the best activity to attract a large group of people. We did start several softball teams. We have several home Bible study programs along with an annual missions conference which would be in direct conflict with a bowling team. Our statement of purpose calls for a climate of spiritual growth and world outreach. These activities would have been deemphasized during the scheduled bowling tournament.

With this simple application of our statement of purpose, "management by objective" we both agreed a bowling team was not the most strategic activity for our church.

With this as our definition of organization, we will restate our statement of purpose:

To glorify God by being mature disciples of Christ by attracting and leading the unsaved to eternal hope through faith in the Lord Jesus Christ, encouraging Christians to consecrate themselves to God, and providing a climate for spiritual growth which equips gifted, Spirit-filled believers for worship and a dynamic ministry, using their gifts in serving our Jerusalem, Judea, and the world.

Now let us move quickly to 1 Corinthians 12:12-31 in which Paul uses the metaphor of the human body to illustrate a practical application of organization. First Corinthians 14:26 states the general purpose of this illustration: "All . . . must be done for the strengthening of the church."

Working with our suggested definition of organization, our statement of purpose, and the biblical illustration of the body, our effort to organize spiritually gifted people becomes a strategic part of being a New Testament church. What an opportunity — to organize your local church to become a place where spiritually gifted people are equipped and serve to glorify God by being mature disciples of Christ.

Before we attempt to organize spiritual gifts into a working model, let's look at some guiding principles.

First Corinthians 12:4-6 is one of several passages that underscores the principle of unity within diversity — different kinds of gifts, but the same Spirit; different kinds of service, but the same Lord; different kinds of working, but the same God. His gifts are the diversified manifestations of His Spirit, even His personal power. God's gifts are not to be separated from His personality. Because of this, there can be no place for boasting, divisions, or rivalry among God's people. The weakest and the apparently lowest of the body is equally important to the function of the whole body.

A second principle is found in 1 Corinthians 13, the "Love" chapter. Without the fruit of the Spirit — LOVE, I am a resounding gong, a clanging cymbal. I am nothing; I have nothing. Spiritual gifts will cease, but love will remain. Ephesians 4:15, which in the context of organizing gifts for ministry states that we are to speak truth in love. Verse 16 seems to state this second principle for organizing gifts for ministry: "From Him the whole body, joined and held together by every supporting ligament, grows and builds itself up in love, as each part does its work."

The first principle is UNITY; the second is LOVE.

Paul states in 1 Corinthians 14:1: "Follow the way of

love and eagerly desire spiritual gifts, especially the gift of prophecy." "But everyone who prophesies speaks to men for their strengthening, encouragement, and comfort" (v. 3). "So it is with you. Since you are eager to have spiritual gifts, try to excel in gifts that build up the church" (v. 12). There is a plan, a strategy for the organization of gifts. This reveals the third principle, the principle of GROWTH—GROWTH that is quality for the church so that the believer is strengthened and comforted. There is also a quantity GROWTH for the church. The church is to plan its activities thinking of the unbeliever (v. 24). There needs to be an attractiveness (not that we're out of our minds) and understanding of truth. Now we would like to share with you a working organizational model which organizes spiritually gifted people for ministry.

First, there needs to be a general grouping of the different offices and ministries of a local church under different spiritual gifts. There will be some overlapping of ministries and gifts. Also this grouping is arbitrary. Another author's grouping may differ from the one in this text, so feel free to customize your chart for your church and its needs.

The following is a suggested list of gifts and ministry. This listing should enable a church to utilize each gifted person in a place of ministry. From this you will be able to evaluate your strengths and weaknesses as a fellowship, and design a recruiting and training program based on spiritually gifted people.

Helps

Boards/Commissions	Music
Officers	Bus driver
Banquet workers	Financial
Librarian	Office help
Nursery coordinator	Hospitality

Missionary
Men's fellowship
Outreach
Sunday School
Audiovisual
Drama
Radio booth
Artistic work
Church services/
    Usher/Greeter
Helper to underprivi-
leged, alcoholics, blind,
deaf

Transportation
Cook
Nurse
Kitchen help
Athletic teams
Maintenance

Serving

Officers
Librarian
Greeter
Building committee
Nursery coordinator
Young people
Missionary circles
Men's fellowship
Music
Kitchen help

Handyman
Carpenter
Church drama productions
Financial
Accounting
Audiovisual
Helper
Office help
Hospitality, meals, lodging

Missionary

Missions board
Missionary financial
support

Outreach
Evangelism

Prophecy

Preaching
Vision

Evangelism
Boards and committees

Adult Sunday School
teacher

Evangelism

Outreach

Crusade work

Prison ministry

Door-to-door visitation

Visitation

Altar counselor

Rescue mission

Telephoning prospects

Intercession

Prayer ministries

Healing ministries

Giving

Church treasurer

Meals and lodging

Support missionaries

Fund raiser

Boards and committees

Sponsor students

Build buildings

Help the needy

Mercy

Altar counselor

Divorce recovery

Drug and alcohol

Abused children

Shut-in

Prison ministry

Blind ·

Bereaved

Cancer care

Mentally ill

Hospital visitation

Convalescent homes

Missions work

Deaf

Knowledge/Wisdom

Research

Youth worker

Marriage enrichment

Altar counselor

Teaching

Counseling

Bible translation

Visitation

Discipleship

Boards and committees

Exhortation

Adult Sunday School
teacher

Discipleship

Visitation

Children's Sunday School
worker
Vacation Bible School
teacher

Counseling
Greeter/Usher
Camp counselor
Boards and committees

Teaching

Discipleship
Youth worker
Camp speaker
Kid's club teacher
Children's Sunday School
teacher

Adult Sunday School
teacher
Home Bible study leader
Board member
Outreach
Visitation

Pastor/Shepherd

Discipleship
Visitation
Training
Youth Work

Home Bible study leader
Outreach
Follow-up
Children's work

Administration

Church office work
Sunday School asst.
Superintendent
Boards and committees
Organizing special events

Sunday School class officer
Financial secretary
Church historian
Library

Discernment

Board member
Recruiter
Counseling
Divorce/recovery

Altar counselor
Visitation
Youth work

Faith

Prayer ministries
Altar counselor

Nominating committee
Board member

Healing ministry   Prayer partner

Music
Choir   Instruments
Band   Orchestra
Choir leader   Sunday School song leader
Worship leader   Bell choir

Miracles
Healing ministries   Prayer ministries
Missions work   Anointing of believers

Craftsmanship
Handyman   Arts and crafts; posters
Building repair   Grounds maintenance
Church office machines

Healing
Healing ministries

Hospitality
The model we are identifying with is presently being used in the Wesleyan Church where it is called GRADE, published by INJOY Ministry out of Bonita, California. Also the Free Methodist Church uses an adaptation of this model called, "Reach Out in Love." The Church of the Nazarene has also published a program written by James L. Garlow, *Partners in Ministry*. The common model found in each of these programs is the dividing of the work of the ministry into four distinctive service areas. The four areas are as follows:

1. The "Andrews" are trained, Spirit-filled believers who take time every week to present the plan of salvation to people in need of Christ.

2. The "Timothys" are trained, Spirit-filled believers who take time every week to love, have fellowship with, and instruct new Christians in successful Christian living.

3. The "Barnabas" or servants are trained, Spirit-filled believers who take time every week to build bridges to the lost through visitation and service ministries within the local church.

4. The "Abrahams" are trained, Spirit-filled believers who take time every week to pray for other workers in the church, the new Christians, and prospects for salvation.

After you establish a general model of ministry, you then begin to place the different gifts under the general division of ministry. The diagram entitled, "Ministry Model" (Illustration 3), illustrates this step. Because the divisions of ministry have such a general definition, it is possible to have the same gift under several divisions.

The last phase for organizing a ministry model is to begin to place names of individuals who scored high in a particular gift area under that area. Again there will be duplication. But after counseling and prayer, one particular gift will surface as the dominant gift. To make this task more functional, we have designed the enclosed "Ministries Gift Questionnaire" (Illustration 4) for your use.

You will also find a "Ministry Opportunities Chart" (Illustration 5) which can be used as a transition activity or aid for the next chapter on commitment.

You may want to consult your denominational discipline or manual to clarify your statement of purpose and organization. One exciting activity is to examine your local church calendar, newsletter, or Sunday bulletin and see if they reflect your statement of purpose.

To conclude this chapter on Organization and Structure,

I would like to share what happened in a church that organized around spiritual gifts.

The church is located in the Portland, Oregon area and is called Faith Evangelical Church. When Pastor Bob came to Faith Church, the attendance at services was as follows: 9:45 Sunday School, 60; 11:00 Morning Worship, 45; and 6:00 P.M. Evening Service, 30.

At the conclusion of a twelve-week course on spiritual gifts, Pastor Bob took the results of the Wesley Spiritual Gifts Questionnaire, reviewed and regrouped the forty adults who took the test according to their gifts. He concluded that Faith Church's gift-mix would not support the traditional 9:45 Sunday School; 11:00 Worship Service and 6:00 Evening Service.

After several weeks of review of their purpose statement, philosophy of ministry, and strengths of their spiritual gift-mix, the church took a bold step and restructured their services. Morning worship was set at 10:30. This became the main flow of their energies, and today the attendance is around 200. The most drastic move was to a Sunday evening Sunday School which has an emphasis of equipping Christians for "being" and "doing." The attendance at the 6:00 P.M. Sunday School is 130. The midweek focus was outreach through small groups with a Children's Club program on Wednesday evening called Christian Life Club. The attendance is 90. There is a 9:30 Sunday morning senior adult Bible study at the church for adults who are not able to attend Sunday evening.

What Faith Church did is a positive application of organizing and structuring a church around spiritual gifts.

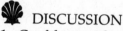 DISCUSSION

1. Could you identify the three guiding principles of organization in the church? Give Bible references to support those principles.

2. Do you agree that management by objectives has a place in the church? Give a reason for your answer.
3. Where do you fit in the ministry model given in chapter 11?

 APPLICATION
After reading this chapter design a ministry model for your church. You may want to talk to your pastor about his/her ideas for a ministry model.

MINISTRY MODEL

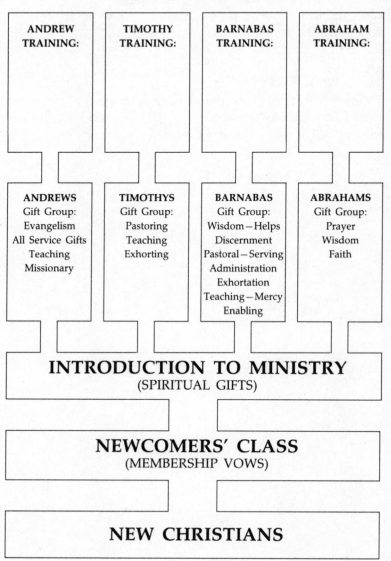

ANDREW TRAINING:	TIMOTHY TRAINING:	BARNABAS TRAINING:	ABRAHAM TRAINING:

ANDREWS	TIMOTHYS	BARNABAS	ABRAHAMS
Gift Group:	Gift Group:	Gift Group:	Gift Group:
Evangelism	Pastoring	Wisdom – Helps	Prayer
All Service Gifts	Teaching	Discernment	Wisdom
Teaching	Exhorting	Pastoral – Serving	Faith
Missionary		Administration	
		Exhortation	
		Teaching – Mercy	
		Enabling	

INTRODUCTION TO MINISTRY
(SPIRITUAL GIFTS)

NEWCOMERS' CLASS
(MEMBERSHIP VOWS)

NEW CHRISTIANS

Illustration 3

Organization and Structure

Name: _____

Phone Number: _____

MINISTRIES GIFTS QUESTIONNAIRE

This works with those using the "Reach Out in Love Program."

Please indicate below as you answer each section (1) the General Ministry in which you would like to serve, (2) the type of service you would like to do in that ministry and (3) the age-level with which you envision yourself serving.

We will use this information to help us in finding a fulfilling ministry for you. You may be contacted about another type of ministry, but your commitment to serve will be the reference point for you to go back to in deciding if that ministry will be one for you to enter.

Just remember—each gift can be used in the various areas and will become the motivational force behind the methods by which you minister in that area.

GENERAL MINISTRY
____ Abraham   Faith, prayer, wisdom, knowledge, leadership
____ Andrew   Evangelism, missionary, teaching, service, healing, miracles, apostleship
____ Timothy   Pastoring, exhortation, teaching, prophecy, leadership
____ Barnabas Wisdom, exhortation, mercy, administration, teaching, helps, discernment, service, giving, pastoring, music, craftsmanship, hospitality

TYPE OF SERVICE
____ Teaching Timothy, Barnabas   Sunday School, Bible study leader, Discipleship group, Care group
____ Outreach Andrew   Usher, Greeter, Caller, Choir, Care groups, Parking attendant
____ Support   Abraham, Barnabas   Prayer, Kitchen help, Choir, Teacher's aide, Caller, Prepare snacks, Audiovisual, Supply supervisor

AGE LEVEL
____ Preschool   ____ Children   ____ Junior high
____ Senior high   ____ Adult (Young, Middle, Senior)

Illustration 4

157

MINISTRY OPPORTUNITIES

TYPE	TEACHING/LEADING	SUPPORT	OUTREACH
Example	Sunday School Teacher Club leader Churchtime worker Youth sponsor	Secretary Usher Administration	Evangelism team
Time Commitment	Classtime Lesson preparation Visitor and absentee follow-up	Service time Some paperwork at home	2–4 hours per week in visitation
Location	Class Home	Church Home	In the community
In-service Training Commitment	Monthly planning/ Training meetings ICL seminar	Monthly planning/ Training meetings Internship	Monthly planning/ Training meetings Special training events Reading
Pre-service Training Commitment	Pre-service training course Internship Reading	Pre-service training course Internship	Pre-service training course Internship Reading

Illustration 5

158

CHAPTER 12

Commitment

C ommitment is a two-way street. There is a commitment to service on the part of the believer, and there is the commitment of the church to equip the believer. The average Christian's commitment will equal the level at which he/she has been recruited. If you buttonhole a worker in the hall, the chances are that he/she will make that type of commitment.

Another interesting fact about commitment is that if your church does not have a statement of purpose which reflects a "theology of service" and commitment to equip the believer for service, you will most likely not be reproducing committed Christians.

First, let's establish the role of the church in relationship to commitment. How does a "theology of service" develop in recruiting and equipping gifted believers for service?

We return to our statement of purpose which was developed in chapter 9 of our text. The purpose of the church is to "provide a climate for spiritual growth which equips gifted, Spirit-filled believers for worship and a dynamic ministry." This means that with conviction and even urgency the church is to win people, build them up, and give them a place to serve. The whole purpose of the Cross is to bring men and women to maturity which includes birth, growth, and service.

Therefore, the local church and its leadership should recruit and train believers, not in a casual way, but because of theological conviction about God, man, and salvation.

There are many strategies for recruiting and training believers. We would suggest that you contact your denominational Christian education leadership for specific information.

Second, let's consider our concept of commitment on the part of the believer. This concept was introduced in the chapter on "Spiritual Gifts in Relation to the Church." It was noted that commitment involves three levels: first, toward God; second, toward the body; and third, toward God's service. It is strategic that these levels are explained as we are challenged to call others to, or make a personal commitment to, Christ and His Church.

Level One. Jesus said that there was no way to God except through Him (John 14:6). As many as believed that He was the Christ were given power to become God's children (1:12). He put commitment to Himself higher than any other relationship (Matt. 10:37-39). Those of us from the Wesleyan tradition are aware of the call to total commitment as expressed in Romans 12:1-2. We believe that after the believer has been cleansed from sin and filled with the Spirit, he/she is at a place of total commitment. This commitment is further described in Ephesians 4, which is a strategic gift passage. Ephesians 4:23-24 says, "To be made new in the attitude of your minds; and to put on the new self, created to be like God in true righteousness and holiness." We have noticed in the Pacific Conference of the Evangelical Church the close proximity of those who enter into the experience of entire sanctification and those who are involved in leadership training.

Level Two. But what about the second level of commitment, the commitment to the body of Christ, the church? Does it really come before service? The answer is yes. One of the few direct measurements of our commitment is that we love one another (John 13:35). In His High Priestly Prayer of John 17, Jesus exclaimed to the Father that men would know that these were His disciples, if they exhibited the same love for one another that existed between the Father and the Son. It is interesting that the Bible has much more to say about our relationship than our service. For our relationship of love is in the context of service to the body. Because I love the body, I attend the service of the fellowship and I am equipped for service.

Level Three. What is the "work of Christ"? This third area of commitment is to Christ's church. The work of Christ could be summarized into two tasks. The first of these is what we call edification, building up the body for service (Eph. 4:11-12). The other part of the work of Christ is to "go and make disciples" (Matt. 28:19). As we build our relationship within the body, on the strong foundation of our relationship to God in Christ, we will discover that there is a base on which we can serve Christ.

The Bible study for this chapter is Exodus 3–4. In these two chapters, we discover an honesty about commitment in service that is frank, yet refreshing. This lesson will give the leader and the learner an opportunity to consider their commitment to ministry. There will also be an opportunity to make a commitment to ministry. As a leader/learner, you will want to observe that Moses was called to do a specific job that was clearly defined. Moses was given what he needed to do the work. Moses committed all he had in order to do what God called him to do.

One of the exciting aspects of these chapters is the way God responded to the excuse Moses offered. Moses was very honest about his feeling of inadequacy. The inspiration of these chapters is God's adequacy for each area of weakness.

A summary chart of this study would look something like this:

Exodus 3:11-12
    Moses: "Who am I that I should go?"
    God: "I will be with you."
Exodus 3:13-14
    Moses: "Then what shall I tell them?"
    God: "I AM has sent you."
Exodus 4:1-2
    Moses: "What if they do not believe me?"
    God: "What is that in your hand?"
    Moses: "A staff."
Exodus 4:10-11
    Moses: "O Lord, I have never been eloquent."
    God: "Who gave man his mouth?"
Exodus 4:13-14
    Moses: "O Lord, please send someone else."
    God (in
      anger):   "What about your brother?"

The first four of these examples show how God can meet any legitimate doubt or fear. The fifth example shows that God is not pleased with a person who has an unwilling spirit toward service.

As a congregation or as an individual, you are challenged to make a three-level commitment. Remember that all the resources of God's power are available in Christ.

Commitment

This chapter on commitment has proposed three concepts: first, commitment from the church and its leader to a theology of service; second, the three levels of commitment on the part of the believer; and third, a Bible study to motivate the believer to make a willing commitment of his/her spiritual gifts. At the conclusion of this chapter you will find a commitment form that may be used at the end of this session (Illustration 6).

Several years ago Dr. Win Arn produced a short film called *The Circus,* with a subtitle "Christ and the Church." There is no dialogue in the film but a climax closing phrase, "It's OK, we can do it," given by the watchman who represents Christ.

The opening scene shows a large open-air circus arena with a watchman leaning against a fence post next to a large chain that blocks the entrance to the arena. The watchman is playing a flute which seems to have a pied piper effect as its sounds are heard by the children throughout the community.

The camera moves from area to area showing children flocking to the circus. The children are excited and cheering as they approach the entrance of the arena. Then their expressions change as they see the entrance chained and padlocked.

The watchman stops playing, looks at the children, then at the chain and lock. The watchman gets up and moves toward the gate as he looks at the children's disappointed yet hopeful faces. With deliberate movements he turns and unlocks the chain and throws open the entrance to the arena. The children cheer and move in masses into the arena.

One boy in a wheelchair is left all alone. The watchman sees him trying hopelessly to get his wheelchair out of a rut. The watchman moves over and helps him through the entrance way.

Inside the arena all the boys and girls are trying on the costumes and totally experiencing all the thrills of a circus. Then comes the time for the big circus parade. The children all run to find their places and costumes for the big event. Every place is taken and all the costumes have been chosen. Then the camera focuses on the boy in the wheelchair off at the side with no costume and no place in the parade.

The watchman reaches into a large costume box and lifts out a drum major hat and baton. He looks at the boy in the wheelchair and gives a gesture of invitation, offering him the hat and baton. The young boy tries to step out of his wheelchair but gives up. The watchman looks up as if in prayer, then invites the boy again to come and be the leader of the parade.

The boy stands, takes a step, then falls to the ground. The boy wipes the dust off his face and again looks at the watchman. The boy tries again to pull himself up. Again the watchman and boy exchange looks. The watchman says in a soft, but steady voice, "It's OK, we can do it." The boy finds the strength for one step, then two, and then rushes to the watchman. The boy puts on the hat and firmly grips the baton. The crowd cheers and the parade begins.

As you have discovered your spiritual gift you may have responded helplessly at first, like Moses, and then felt God's help and strength, even as the helpless child in the story.

I would like to remind you as you make your commitment to Christ, to the body, and to ministry that Jesus in a very real way says, "It's OK, we can do it."

DISCUSSION
1. Write in your own words the three levels of commitment shared in chapter 12.

2. Make a comparison of your feelings of inadequacy and those of Moses.

3. Do you agree that ministry within the local church is a spiritual necessity? Give a reason for your response.

 APPLICATION

Within the next two days fill out the Spiritual Gifts Commitment sheet, Illustration 6. Now make an appointment with your pastor to talk about your spiritual gifts and ministry in your local church.

SPIRITUAL GIFTS COMMITMENT

Name _____

Address _____

Phone # _____

I believe, as a result of studying gifts, praying about my gift, and the results of the questionnaire, that God has gifted me in the following areas:

PRIMARY	SECONDARY
1.	4.
2.	5.
3.	6.

I dedicate these to His service within the fellowship of this church. In those cases where I'm not sure where God has gifted me, I would like the opportunity to try out those gifts. I am available to be called on by the leadership of this church for the exercise of my gift(s).

Signed _____

Illustration 6

BIBLIOGRAPHY

REFERENCES CITED

Flynn, Leslie B. *19 Gifts of the Spirit*. Wheaton, Ill.: Victor Books, 1981.

Garlow, James L. *Partners in Ministry*. Kansas City, Mo.: Beacon Hill Press, 1981.

Glaphré. *When the Pieces Don't Fit . . . God Makes the Difference*. Grand Rapids: Zondervan, 1984.

Godbey, W.B. *Spiritual Gifts and Graces*. Cincinnati: M.W. Knapp, 1895.

Hogue, Wilson T. *The Holy Spirit, a Study*. Chicago: William B. Rose, 1916.

Jones, E. Stanley. *A Song of Ascents*. Nashville: Abingdon, 1968.

Kinghorn, Kenneth C. *Gifts of the Spirit*. Nashville: Abingdon, 1976.

Purkiser, W.T. *The Gifts of the Spirit*. Kansas City, Mo.: Beacon Hill Press, 1975.

Swindoll, Charles R. *Growing Strong in the Seasons of Life*. Portland, Oregon: Multnomah Press, 1983.

Wagner, C. Peter. *Your Spiritual Gifts Can Help Your Church Grow*. Glendale, Calif.: Regal, 1974.

Wesley, John. *The Works of John Wesley*. Grand Rapids: Zondervan, 1872.

DATE DUE

NOV 2 1 2008			
NOV 2 _ 2008			

#47-0108 Peel Off Pressure Sensitive